A
NEW
CREATION

A NEW CREATION

A Study of Salvation

Homer G. Rhea

PATHWAY PRESS
CLEVELAND, TENNESSEE 37311

Library of Congress Catalog Card Number: 83-62003

ISBN: 0-87148-630-X

Copyright © 1996 by Pathway Press
Cleveland Tennessee 37311
All Rights Reserved
Printed in the United States of America

To my wife, Jimmie,
who is my strongest supporter;
my sons, Ronnie and Paul,
whose research on this book
was invaluable to me;
and
my daughters, Donna and Lynn,
who add much joy to my life.

Table of Contents

Table of Contents

COURSE INSTRUCTIONS

WELCOME TO A NEW EXPERIENCE IN BIBLE STUDY

This is a self-study course which has been designed to aid you in discovering for yourself life-changing truths from God's Word. The unique format of this text makes it both a study manual and a resource book that you will want to keep on your library shelf for future reference.

READ THESE INSTRUCTIONS CAREFULLY BEFORE YOU BEGIN

Here are a few simple guidelines to follow as you study this course:

1. Try to arrange for a *specific* time each day for your study. Find a quiet place where there are as few distractions as possible.

2. Always keep your Bible handy for ready reference. (Some courses may require the use of a tape player also.)

3. Read each chapter section thoroughly, trying to understand clearly what you are reading.

4. When you come to one of the boxes entitled "Understanding What You Read," stop reading and answer the questions in the box. Check your answers, and when you are certain that you understand each question, begin reading the next chapter section.

5. When you have finished reading the entire chapter and have correctly responded to the questions in each of the boxes, take the Self-Check Test at the end of the chapter. Answer the questions without referring back to the text.

6. Check your answer to the Self-Check Test with the key in the back of the book. Look up the answer to any questions that you may have answered incorrectly.

7. After completing and correcting the Self-Check Test, you are ready to go on to the next chapter.

INTRODUCTION

When a person comes to Christ and accepts Him as Savior, he becomes a new creation. Paul wrote, "Therefore, if anyone is in Christ, he is a new creation; the old has gone, the new has come!" (2 Corinthians 5:17, *NIV*). This course deals with some of the basic doctrines of salvation, some thoughts about lifestyle and discipleship, as well as a brief look at the afterlife.

As you study this course, we hope that you will gain a better understanding of what has happened in your life and of what is expected of you now that you have started on this new journey. You now have new directions, new goals, and new objectives. You have embarked upon the most exciting adventure known to man. We hope that this book will help you navigate the course of your life successfully and safely secure the shores of eternity.

This course is based on the Bible. During your study you will notice that it contains many references to chapters and verses in the Bible. You will find your studying much more enjoyable and beneficial if you take time to look up these verses and read what they say. The verses printed in the text of this course are taken from the *New International Version* (*NIV*), *The New King James Version* (*NKJV*), the *New American Standard Bible* (*NASB*), *The New Testament in the Language of Today* (BECK), as well as the time-honored King James Version.

At the end of each chapter you will find the words "For Further Study." The books listed in this section contain helpful information about the subject you have studied in the chapter. You may wish to buy these books for your personal library. Most of them are available through any Christian bookstore.

May the Lord add His blessings to this course, and may your journey be most pleasant.

1

MAN'S DILEMMA: A NEED FOR CHANGE

Man—created in the image of God. How can this be? Man is selfish; man is weak; man is evil. God is holy; God is powerful; God is love. But the Bible says, "God created man in his own image" (Genesis 1:27). Could it be that man is not what he once was?

What Man Was

Creation. "In the beginning God created the heaven and the earth" (Genesis 1:1). God surveyed His work and was pleased. He saw the earth in all its beauty: the lush vegetation, the sparkling rivers, the rolling hills. He looked on with pleasure while His newly created animals played in the velvety fields.

Man. But who would rule His creation? This was one of the reasons man was created. He was formed from the dust of the earth. Years later Christ would mix that same dust with His spittle and use it to give sight to the eyes of the blind man (John 9:1-7). God's newly formed man was not even equal to the animals until God breathed life into him. This life gave man intelligence, reason, and individuality. It enabled man to worship his Creator. And God was pleased. This was His greatest creation.

Garden. God placed man in a garden He had prepared for him. Here the man's every need was met. He was given an abundant water supply. Food was plentiful. God had provided all kinds of trees with fruit that was good to eat. These trees and their fruit gave the garden beauty beyond belief. The man had no need of shelter, for no animal would harm him and no rain fell at that time (Genesis 2:5, 6). He needed only to take care of his paradise and enjoy it.

Companion. God saw one need that had not yet been met: man's need for companionship. He brought all of the animals before man, but none was found to be a suitable helper for him. God then created woman to be a companion to man.

God blessed the man and woman and told them to multiply and fill the earth. They were happy, ruling God's creation together, and God was pleased. He came down and walked in the garden with them, and they enjoyed fellowship with Him.

Free Will. The Lord instructed Adam and Eve that they could eat the fruit of any tree in the garden except the one in the middle, the tree of the knowledge of good and evil. The Bible does not tell us why God put this tree in the garden. Certainly He had man's best interest in mind when He did. Perhaps it was the possibility of choosing evil that assured man of his free will.

Free will allows man to choose between good and evil. God required obedience of man; yet, he could choose to disobey God. What would happen to man if his interests went against the plans of God?

UNDERSTANDING WHAT YOU READ

Note: *You may want to use a pencil or write your answers on another sheet of paper in case corrections must be made.*

In this section you should have learned that all of God's creation was originally good.

1. Man was created to _____ God's creation.
2. After creating man God placed him in _____.
3. God saw man was lonely so He created _____.
4. The tree whose fruit God forbade Adam and Eve to eat was _____.

Answers, page 178.

What Happened to Man

Man became a different person. A person of fears and limitations. A person who was a horrid sight to God and a menace to himself. A person who was doomed to die.

Temptation. Man suffered this change because he sinned against God. Adam's and Eve's sin began, commonly enough, with a temptation. Satan came to the woman in the form of a serpent to beguile her. He showed her the fruit of the tree of knowledge of good and evil and tempted her to eat it. Satan assured her that if she ate of the tree she would not die, as God had told her. He suggested rather that she would become like God, knowing good and evil.

Christ's Temptation. Christ was later tempted in much the same manner. Satan approached Him after He had been fasting for many days. He suggested that Christ turn the stones to bread to end His hunger (Matthew 4:1-11). Satan tempted Eve, suggesting that the fruit was good to eat. Eve, however, was not in dire need of food as was Christ. She gave in to the temptation; Christ did not.

Christ was also offered great personal gain. All the kingdoms of the world could have been His; He had but to bow down and worship Satan. Eve was offered the knowledge of good and evil for her personal gain. She lacked the strength to resist; Christ, although physically weak, resisted the temptation.

The Fall. Eve, although in perfect health and in a perfect environment, was not satisfied. She sought independence from God. She sought to lay claim to her own soul. In seeking what she thought was best for her husband and herself, she rebelled against God.

Although Eve was the first to partake of the fruit, she does not bear sole blame for the Fall. This was the first defense Adam pleaded when confronted by the Lord after the sin. But God did not accept this excuse, and neither should we. Adam was "with her" (Genesis 3:6); yet, there is no indication that he tried to keep her from eating the fruit. Neither is there any indication that he resisted at all when she gave it to him. He willingly accepted the fruit and ate. They both bear the blame for the Fall, for they committed the sin together in body and in spirit.

Adam and Eve lusted for things they did not have and did not need. Centuries later Jesus addressed this subject. He said, "Whosoever looketh on a woman to lust after her hath committed adultery with her already in his heart" (Matthew 5:28). John added, "Whosoever hateth his brother is a murderer" (1 John 3:15). Scripture is saying that when a man chooses to do wrong, he is guilty of that wrong. It is not necessary to carry out a sinful act to be guilty of it. The sin is committed in the heart before any action is taken. This was the case with Adam and Eve. It was at the point where they thought of eating the fruit for their own gain that they rebelled against God. They disobeyed God in their heart before they ever tasted the fruit.

God was no longer pleased with man. He descended from heaven one evening and found the man and the woman hiding from Him (Genesis 3:8). They were ashamed of their nakedness, they said, and had sewn fig leaves together to clothe themselves. The Lord asked how they knew they were naked. The man admitted he had eaten of the forbidden tree, but he blamed the woman for his actions. Here self-concern was more and more evident. Adam was worried about himself and no longer committed to God. Eve promptly passed the blame on to the serpent. Men have been rationalizing their wrongdoing ever since.

The Curse. God listened to their account of the wrong done and heard the pleas of the guilty. He then decided what punishment the serpent and the unhappy couple deserved.

First, God cursed the serpent, causing him to crawl on his belly and eat dust. Then He issued the serpent his ultimate doom: to be crushed by the One whose heel he strikes (Genesis 3:14,15). This curse refers to the crucifixion of Christ. Satan thought he had won a victory in the death of Jesus. Actually that death sealed his fate and gave God the ultimate triumph.

Next, God spoke of the curse upon the woman. Her pain would be greatly increased in bearing children (Genesis 3:16). She would also be put under the subjection of her husband. He would rule over her.

Turning to the man, God cursed the ground so it would be unresponsive to the man's toil (Genesis 3:17-19). Only through hard labor and sweat would man feed his family. By producing thorns and thistles the ground would fight him in this struggle. God included in His curse of man the coming of death. Thus, after a lifetime of struggle with the dust of the earth, man will always lose and return to the ground.

God cursed the serpent, the woman, and the man, and that curse touched everything on earth in some way. The Apostle Paul said the whole creation is groaning as though suffering the pain of childbirth (see Romans 8:22). If we look around, we shall see the pain; let us keep looking, and we shall feel the pain. Man has polluted this beautiful planet, its atmosphere, and its inhabitants. He has caused the extinction and near extinction of many species that once flourished.

Since the Fall of Man, death has invaded this world. Everything on earth began to decay, and all things living were assigned a time to die. The effects of death are seen in the soil. The ground from which all living beings came is subject to death when used continuously for the same crop. Death finds its way into the world through the environment. Disease, famine, and natural disasters bring death not only to man but to all living things, to the guilty and to the innocent.

The last phase of the curse placed upon the man and woman was exile from the garden. They were barred from the only home they had ever known. Their perfect environment was taken away. This punishment was necessary. It would have been harmful for man if he had eaten of the tree of life in his fallen state (Genesis 3:22). God had to prevent this at the cost of closing His beautiful garden to the creatures for whom He had so carefully made it. Sin brought a state of death, of decay, of depravity. If man had eaten of the tree of life in this state, he would have lived forever in this pitiful condition. There would have been no salvation, no hope.

No hope? No hope for Adam and Eve? No hope for any man? What impact could the sin of one man thousands of years past have on what man is today?

UNDERSTANDING WHAT YOU READ

In this section you should have learned the nature of the Fall of Man and how he was cursed when he fell.

1. Satan came to Eve in the form of a _____.

2. Adam and Eve were ashamed because _____.

3. First God cursed _____, then _____, and then _____.

4. God exiled Adam and Eve from the garden to prevent them from eating _____.

Answers, page 178.

What Man Is Today

Compared to what man was and what God intends him to be, today man is an abomination: disgusting in the sight of nature, in the sight of God, and in his own sight. In *The Problem of Pain*, C. S. Lewis addressed this thought. He wrote: "Man is now a horror to God and to himself and a creature ill-adapted to the universe not because God made him so but because he has made himself so by the abuse of his free will." Man has become a curse, a pollutant, a malignant growth on the creation of God.

To Animals. Man has been terrorizing animals throughout history. At one time buffalo covered the Great Plains of western America, but killing them became a sport to men, and they were brought to the edge of extinction. Many species have suffered such a fate and worse. The list is long. Too long! How could the animal kingdom not live in fear of man? How could it help but react as T.H. White described in *The Once and Future King*? One of his creatures says that when a man went "for a walk beside the river, not only would the birds fly from him and the beasts run away from him, but the very fish would dart to the other side." He adds, "They don't do this for each other."

To God. Man has become a horrible sight to God because he is unholy and totally lacking in the character God intended him to have. He has become dependent upon himself, not upon God. He has lifted himself up, not God. The qualities God holds so dear, he has forsaken. He has marred God's creation and become a threat to his fellow man.

To Himself. Of all the terrors man faces, the worst is himself. He must face the peril of living in a society with himself, a society that is self-centered. Take the case of Society Kid Hogan. Red Smith tells about him in *To Absent Friends From Red Smith*. Hogan was a lightweight boxer and an avid fan of horse racing. He was hurrying through the Illinois Central pedestrian tunnel under Michigan Avenue on June 9, 1930, when a man in the crowd put a gun to another man's head and shot him. Hogan kept right on walking. When the police asked him later why he didn't stop, he said, "The last train was leaving for the racetrack." Hogan's attitude is more typical of men in general than we like to admit.

Or take the case of man's constant fear of war. This gruesome game men have improved upon for thousands of years now threatens to destroy the entire human race. There is no place to hide.

Or take the case of crime. Murderers and rapists rule the streets of many cities so that it is dangerous to go out at night alone. Policemen cannot enforce the law when there is not room for new prisoners in our overcrowded jails. There is no place to hide.

Or take the matter of starving people. Those who have food trade it, hoard it, or waste it, but seldom give it to those in such dire need. There is no place to hide because we are hiding from ourselves.

Death. Man is a dying creature. He is subjected to death physically, spiritually, and morally. From the time of his birth his body begins the slow journey to death. There is no alternate route. The writer of Hebrews declared, "It is appointed unto men once to die, but after this the judgment" (Hebrews 9:27).

From the time of his first sin man began a journey away from God. Thus, he is faced continually with spiritual death. Paul stated it this way: "For all have sinned, and come short of the glory of God" (Romans 3:23). Because man has missed the mark, his character is not what God intends it to be. He is morally weak.

The quality so obviously missing is love. Love has never been manifested in mankind as a whole. Yet Jesus said that love is the most important trait. "And Jesus answered him, The first of all the commandments is, Hear, O Israel; The Lord our God is one Lord: And thou shalt love the Lord thy God with all thy heart, and with all thy soul, and with all thy mind, and with all thy strength: this is the first commandment. And the second is like, namely this, Thou shalt love thy neighbour as thyself. There is none other commandment greater than these" (Mark 12:29-31). Without love all else is nothing. Whatever good qualities a man may show, they fall short if not based on love.

The sin of Adam brought death into the world—not just for Adam, but for all men. Listen to the Apostle Paul: "Wherefore, as by one man sin entered into the world, and death by sin; and so death passed upon all men, for that all have sinned" (Romans 5:12). "For the wages of sin is death" (Romans 6:23). Some persons question how the sin of one man could doom the whole human race. Others respond by saying that since we were all there in the body of Adam, we took part in the sin. Still others point out that Adam was the head of the race, and thus represented all mankind. For this reason men can be restored to fellowship with God. When Lucifer fell, it was by his choice and all of the angels who accompanied him chose to do so. Men, however, were doomed by one man. It was not as though each man had rebelled against God. The choice was made for the rest by the head of the race: Adam. When men reach the age of accountability, they may turn to God in repentance and faith and be restored to favor with Him.

Man was cast out of Eden into the world, which Satan controlled. When Adam and Eve had children, they were born of the world. Their children's children and all generations till today were born of this world. This means, of course, that man is today born with the hand of death upon him. The wages of sin is still death.

UNDERSTANDING WHAT YOU READ

In this section you should have learned that man is a horrible sight to nature, God, and himself and that because of sin he is subject to death.

1. _____ flee from the presence of men.

2. All men have been appointed a time to _____.

3. Because we do not have _____, our morals are as nothing.

Answers, page 178.

Before the Fall man could choose to obey God or not to obey Him. When man sinned, he lost the ability to obey God and became a slave to disobedience.

Jesus said, "Whosoever committeth sin is the servant of sin" (John 8:34). Paul wrote, "Know ye not, that to whom ye yield yourselves servants to obey, his servants ye are to whom ye obey; whether of sin unto death, or of obedience unto righteousness?" (Romans 6:16). So, man lost the ability not to sin. This is the state of need in which he finds himself today.

In the next chapter we shall look at the provision God has made to meet this need.

FOR FURTHER STUDY

Lewis, C. S. *The Problem of Pain.* New York, NY: Macmillan, 1962.

SELF-CHECK TEST

After you have read Chapter 1 and looked up the verses in the Bible, you should take this brief self-check test. Answer the questions without referring back to the text.

Multiple Choice

Choose the answer that best completes the following statements and circle it in pencil or use another sheet of paper to record your answers.

1. God created man . . .
    a. to terrorize the animals.
    b. in His own image.
    c. to rule over the woman.
    d. in the garden of Eden.

2. Man's job in the garden was . . .
    a. to feed the animals.
    b. to plant trees.
    c. to kill insects.
    d. to take care of the garden.

3. To satisfy man's need for companionship God first . . .
    a. brought the animals before him.
    b. created a woman.
    c. exiled him from the garden.
    d. built a temple.

4. The doctrine of free will includes . . .
    a. slavery.
    b. violence.
    c. peace of mind.
    d. the possibility of choosing evil.

5. In disobeying God Adam and Eve sought to lay claim to . . .
    a. the garden.
    b. the animals.
    c. their own soul.
    d. each other.

6. Upon being charged of sin by God, Adam's first defense of himself was . . .
    a. to blame the serpent.
    b. to blame God for putting that tree there.
    c. to blame the woman.
    d. to show God how the fruit benefited him.

7. God cursed the serpent, the woman and the man but that curse affected . . .
    a. all living beings.
    b. no other animals.
    c. the birds and no other animals.
    d. the amount of rainfall per year.

8. Man was sent away from the garden . . .
   a. as punishment.
   b. as an example to other animals.
   c. to prevent him from eating from the tree of
      life.
   d. to prevent them from eating of the fruit of
      the tree of knowledge of good and evil
      again.

9. Man is a horrible sight to . . .
   a. God.
   b. himself.
   c. nature.
   d. all of the above.

10. The moral quality man has never totally
    achieved is . . .
    a. love.
    b. courage.
    c. peace.
    d. valor.

When you have marked the answers that you believe to be correct for these ten questions, look up the answers in the back of the book. If you got at least eight answers right, you may proceed to Chapter 2. If you had three or more wrong answers, you should read this lesson again, retake the test, and then go ahead to Chapter 2.

2

GOD'S PROVISION: AN OPPORTUNITY TO CHANGE

M an was in a desperate state. He had spat in the face of God, denied Him, rejected Him, and rebelled against Him, but God still loved man. God loved man so much that He sent His only Son to be murdered by ungrateful men, so that those same ungrateful men might be welcomed back into the kingdom of the loving Father.

The Loving Father

One of the parables Jesus told during His ministry was that of a wealthy father and his two sons (Luke 15). The younger son was bored and wanted a change. He approached his father one day, asking for his inheritance immediately. He was not willing to wait until the death of his father for that to which he was entitled. By law he was to inherit one-third of his father's estate because he was the younger of two sons. (The firstborn received a double portion.) The father consented, although he did not want his son to leave him.

The young man journeyed into a distant land and began living a wild life. He had plenty of money, so he had plenty of friends and plenty of fun. But the money was soon gone and so were his friends and his fun. A famine came into the land, and the young man found himself in need with no one to help him. He was alone and beyond his father's help.

The young man was given work feeding pigs, but he still went hungry. Near starvation, he came to his senses and remembered that his father's workers had food to spare. He decided to return to his father and ask to be taken in as one of his hired servants. So, he began the long journey back to his father.

The young man's father had been hoping and praying that his son would come back to him. He had watched day after day in hope of seeing his son coming home. At last he saw him coming and ran to meet him while he was still a long way off. He welcomed his son back with a kiss.

Here Jesus was showing us the love of our Father in heaven. God is not content to sit and wait for us to come knocking at His door. He runs to meet us, welcomes us with a kiss, and then brings us in. God so loved us that He Himself reached out for us; He did not send a messenger. It is He who takes the first step toward saving men. Adam and Eve hid from God in the garden after they had sinned, but God came to them. They did not seek Him; He sought them. He loves us and is seeking to bring us back to Him.

The prodigal son asked his father to be taken back as a hired servant. The father answered him by bringing him the best robe (signifying honor), a ring (signifying authority), and shoes (signifying sonship, for the slaves did not wear shoes).

The son thought he could earn his way back into his father's house by offering to be a hired servant, but he could not because sonship was the gift of the father free of charge. It was a gift of love. Our Heavenly Father gives us sonship. We have but to receive it.

The father prepared a celebration for the returned son, but jealousy prevented the elder son from going in and taking part. He had stayed and worked for his father while the younger was away, and he felt cheated. So, the father went out to bring his oldest son into the house. He explained to his son that all he had was at his disposal all along. He asked this son to come in and celebrate, saying that the son who had been dead was alive.

As the father in the parable restored his prodigal son, so the Heavenly Father restores His wandering children who come home.

UNDERSTANDING WHAT YOU READ

Note: *You may want to use a pencil or write your answers on another sheet of paper in case corrections must be made.*

In this section you should have learned that our Heavenly Father reaches out to us to bring us to salvation.

1. In the Parable of the Prodigal Son, the younger son was given the job _____ of after he had used up his money.

2. The younger son chose to return to his father as a _____.

3. When he saw his son coming, the father _____.

4. Having restored him to his house, the father said that the son who had been dead was _____.

Answers, page 178.

The Greatest Gift

The greatest gift a man can give is that which costs the greatest sacrifice. (Compare 2 Samuel 24:18-25.) A generous man may give up something he loves; a truly generous man may lay down his life for a friend; but who would sacrifice the life of his son for the benefit of those who despise him? God loved men so much that He gave them His Son to be hated and killed, that those same men might be saved from destruction. This is love. God is love.

Jesus told the story of a man who planted a vineyard, fenced it in, and built a tower and a winepress. He left this well-equipped vineyard to a group of men and went to live in a distant land. (Read Matthew 21:33-46; Mark 12:1-9; Luke 20:9-19.)

This story refers to Isaiah 5:1-7 where it is said "For the vineyard of the Lord of hosts is the house of Israel" (Isaiah 5:7). Those to whom He was speaking knew immediately that Jesus was referring to this passage. They understood that the vineyard He spoke of was the house of Israel: the keepers of the vineyard represented the religious leaders of that day; the plants in the vineyard were meant to be the people of Israel; and the owner represented God. That the vineyard was well-equipped shows us that God will abundantly supply the tools we need to complete the tasks He gives us.

When the fruit was ripe, the owner sent his servants back to the vineyard to get the share of fruit that belonged to him. When they arrived, the servants were abused by the men who had been left in charge. Some were beaten, some stoned, and some killed. Those that survived were sent away empty-handed. The owner sent more servants to receive what was his, but they were given the same treatment.

The servants Jesus spoke of were the prophets, whom God had repeatedly sent and whom man had repeatedly rejected. This portion of the story tells of God's love for man. He must have loved these rebellious men a great deal. He sent men who loved Him and obeyed Him to their death in an attempt to let these rebels come back to Him so that they might not lose the vineyard. God's patience with men is thus revealed. Although men abuse those whom God sends, and even God Himself, He is willing to give them another chance.

The owner did not know what to do next. He had tried everything. There was only one thing left and that was to send his son. He thought those men might respect his son, but he knew it was a dangerous mission. So, the son went to the vineyard to receive his father's payment. The keepers of the vineyard saw their opportunity to get the vineyard for themselves by killing the son of the owner. So, they killed the owner's only son, the son the owner loved so greatly.

God loves us so much that He sent His Son, knowing that He would be killed. This action shows God's love for us more than any action He has ever taken. To give up His Son to save a race that deserves destruction is the greatest gift imaginable. There is no gift greater. There is no love greater.

To end the parable, Jesus vowed destruction for the corrupt religious leaders so that the justice of God would be satisfied. Men will take advantage of the love and patience of God, but in the end judgment will come to them.

UNDERSTANDING WHAT YOU READ

In this section you should have learned of the vastness of God's love as shown by Him sending His son to die that we might be saved.

1. In the parable told here, the vineyard represents _____.

2. After sending servants twice to receive payment, the owner decided to send _____.

3. The keepers of the vineyard _____ the owner's son.

4. At the end of the parable Jesus vowed destruction for the corrupt _____.

Answers, page 176.

Come to the Feast

The Father reaches out. "Come to supper. To you it is free. I have paid the price." For the Father gave His Son so that all men might come to the feast. The price has been paid, and the Father stretches out His lengthy arms to welcome us to a free and everlasting supper.

Jesus told the Parable of the Great Supper (Luke 14). The host invited many to come to his home and dine. The invitations were well received, and all those invited seemed eager for the day of the feast to arrive. However, when that day did arrive, those who had been invited all made excuses, saying they could not come. Much angered by this, the host instructed his servant to go to the poor, the lame, and the blind and invite them to the feast. Being truly hungry, these people gladly accepted the kind offer and immediately went to partake of the feast.

In this Parable of the Great Supper Jesus was speaking to a great extent about Himself. He was the invitation to the feast. When we accept Him, we may enjoy the feast the Father offers us. The people originally invited to God's feast were the Jews. For centuries they eagerly awaited the day when the Messiah would come; but when that day finally came, they rejected the invitation. They rejected Christ. God took His invitation elsewhere. The poor, the lame, and the blind represent those who accepted Jesus: the tax collectors, adulterers, and other sinners shunned by the Jews. Those who were truly hungry found food. Those who were truly thirsty found drink.

The excuses made by those first invited to the feast point out several things that can keep men from receiving Jesus, the greatest gift they could ever receive. The first excuse given dealt with business interests. This man had bought a piece of ground and needed to go see it. He let matters of business keep him from the feast. The second man excused himself because he had just bought a team of oxen, and he needed to try them out. Many times we get caught up with new and exciting things, so much that we miss the feast of God. The last man said that he had recently been married so he could not come. In this instance a perfectly good and wholesome thing, marriage, held sacred in the eyes of God since Adam and Eve, kept a man from responding to God's call. The excuses given all seemed valid to those who gave them, and that is what makes them so dangerous.

The host had brought in all the poor, lame, and blind that could be found; and yet, there was still plenty of room. He told his servant to go out to the suburbs and bring the people he found there to his feast. He then pronounced judgment on those who had refused to come, saying that none of them would taste of his supper.

There is room at the feast of God for all who will come. The invitation to those from the suburbs represents the call of the Gentiles. There are no men in this world God will not welcome, for He is calling all men to accept Christ and partake of His everlasting feast. Those who do not accept Christ do not taste of the delights God has prepared for them. Jesus is the door by which one may enter the banquet hall.

The feast Jesus was speaking of in this parable provides for our past, our present, and our future. When we accept God's invitation and eat of this great supper, our yesterdays are forgotten. We are filled and are no longer burdened with past hunger. That would mean very little, however, if our tomorrows were not also provided for. We would despair if it were only a temporary solution, but happily the feast is always before us. We are able to partake of the goodness and mercy of God, because it is always available to us. Last, the feast is now. God intended for the Christian life to be a happy life. He wants us fully to enjoy all of the pleasures He has provided for us. We have but to reach out and take from God, and His goodness and mercy will fill us, so that we overflow with joy.

The feast of God is now and forever. "Surely goodness and mercy shall follow me all the days of my life: and I will dwell in the house of the Lord for ever" (Psalm 23:6).

Come to the feast. The door has been opened to all who will enter.

UNDERSTANDING WHAT YOU READ

In this section you should have learned that the Father completes the process of salvation by saving us and bringing us into the glories of a Christian life.

1. When Christ came to the Jews, they _____.
2. The first excuse given by the invited guests was one of a _____ nature.
3. After Jesus pointed out that salvation was available for even the lowliest of Jews, He went on to include _____.
4. God intended for the Christian life to be a _____ life.

Answers, page 176.

FOR FURTHER STUDY

Sauer, Erich. *The Dawn of World Redemption.* Grand Rapids, MI: Eerdmans, 1951.

Sauer, Erich. *The Triumph of the Crucified.* Grand Rapids, MI: Eerdmans, 1951.

SELF-CHECK TEST

After you have read Chapter 2 and looked up the verses in the Bible, you should take this brief self-check test. Answer the questions without referring back to the text.

Choose the answer that best completes the following statements and circle it in pencil or use another sheet of paper to record your answers.

1. By law the younger of two sons received . . .
   a. one-half of his father's estate.
   b. none of his father's estate.
   c. one-third of his father's estate.
   d. all of his father's estate.

2. After Adam and Eve sinned, they hid from God, but . . .
   a. God came down and sought them out.
   b. God struck them dead.
   c. God ignored them.
   d. God sent the serpent to bite them.

3. The shoes the father brought his son in the parable of the Prodigal Son signified . . .
   a. that he was accepted as a hired servant.
   b. honor.
   c. authority.
   d. that his sonship was returned to him.

4. When the older son would not go in to the
feast, the father . . .
   a. had him flogged.
   b. went out to get him.
   c. locked the door.
   d. moved the party outside.

5. A truly great gift . . .
   a. is a great sacrifice.
   b. is big.
   c. is given because one has to.
   d. is always asked for beforehand.

6. When God gives us a task, He always . . .
   a. demands that we do it His way.
   b. completes the task Himself.
   c. assumes the task will not be done.
   d. gives us enough tools to complete the task.

7. The act of God that showed His love for men
most was . . .
   a. the deluge of Noah's day.
   b. sending His only Son to die for us.
   c. cursing the serpent.
   d. giving man dominion over His creation.

8. At the feast of the Heavenly Father . . .
   a. there is not room for everyone.
   b. the Gentiles are turned away.
   c. all are welcome.
   d. only Jews are welcome.

9. Not included in the excuses given by the men
   who had been invited was . . .
   a. business.
   b. new and exciting things.
   c. sickness.
   d. good things.

10. The feast of God includes . . .
   a. the future.
   b. good things offered to us now.
   c. the removal of past hunger.
   d. all of the above.

When you have marked the answers that you believe to be correct for these ten questions, look up the answers in the back of the book. If you got at least eight answers right, you may proceed to Chapter 3. If you had three or more wrong answers, you should read this lesson again, retake the tests and then go ahead to Chapter 3.

3

CHRIST'S ATONEMENT: THE MEANS TO CHANGE

One of the great English novels, George Eliot's *Romola*, centers around a Greek man named Tito Melema. Along with his father, he had been attacked by pirates in the Mediterranean. When Tito managed to escape, his father gave him some precious stones. Tito was to use these gems to buy back his father from slavery when he reached a place of safety. But the selfish and pleasure-loving son used those precious stones for his own comfort and his own gain. He abandoned and forgot his father who was held in slavery.

Jesus Christ did just the opposite for us. Faithful friend that He is, He died on the cross to pay the price for our redemption. As someone has well said, "Before time commenced its solemn march, Divine love considered man's ruined condition and resolved not to spare the greatest gift which either time could know or eternity produce." The Father gave His Son, and the Son willingly laid down His life that men might be redeemed from their sins.

The Importance of Christ's Death

The importance of Christ's death is seen in the great amount of space given to it in the Bible. As early as the third chapter of Genesis the subject is introduced. The Lord said to the serpent, "And I will put enmity between you and the woman, and between your seed and her Seed; He shall bruise your head, and you shall bruise His heel" (v. 15, *NKJV*). The prophecy referred to the crucifixion of Christ. Satan would view it as his greatest victory, when in reality it would be his ultimate defeat.

The death of Christ was symbolized in the Jewish Festival of Passover. The festival celebrated the Exodus account of the Passover lamb, whose blood was sprinkled over the doorposts of Egypt. The blood on the doorposts was a covering that protected the Hebrews from the death angel. Likewise, the shed blood of Jesus means salvation for those who trust in Him. Peter wrote, "You were not redeemed with corruptible things, like silver or gold . . . but with the precious blood of Christ, as of a lamb without blemish and without spot" (1 Peter 1:18, 19, *NKJV*).

Several Old Testament acts typify Christ's death. Two of them are Isaac's sacrifice (Genesis 22:1-19; Hebrews 11:17-19) and the lifting up of the brass serpent (Numbers 21:4-9; John 3:14, 15).

Many of the prophets and poets of the Old Testament wrote of the Lord's death (read Psalm 22; Isaiah 50; 52; 53).

R. A. Torrey said that the death of Jesus is mentioned directly more than 175 times in the New Testament. When Jesus was an infant, His mother was told of the sorrow she could expect (Luke 2:35). At the beginning of His ministry Jesus was introduced by John the Baptist as the Lamb of God (John 1:29, 36). The Gospels give much attention to this theme.

In *What the Bible Says,* Lewis Drummond observed: "In any other kind of biography one would hardly expect to commence reading about the closing week of the subject's life when barely halfway through the book. Yet in the Gospels this is precisely the case. It is one illustration of the supreme place given to this wonderful theme in the mind and purpose of God as well as in the preaching of the church."

The importance of Christ's death is seen in the interest shown in it. Peter wrote that the Old Testament prophets pondered and explored this theme. "Concerning this salvation, the prophets, who spoke of the grace that was to come to you, searched intently and with the greatest care, trying to find out the time and circumstances to which the Spirit of Christ in them was pointing when he predicted the sufferings of Christ and the glories that would follow" (1 Peter 1:10, 11, *NIV*). In the next verse Peter said that "even angels long to look into these things" (v. 12, *NIV*). When Moses and Elijah appeared with Christ on the Mount of Transfiguration, they talked with Him about His death (Luke 9:30, 31). John wrote that the great anthem of heaven and of the universe will be a tribute to the slain Lamb (Revelation 5:8-14).

The importance of Christ's death is seen in that it was the reason He came into the world. He lived a perfect life and gave the greatest moral and ethical teachings known to mankind. Yet, this was not the ultimate reason for His earthly existence. He came to pay the price of redemption for mankind. He said it best: "The Son of man came not to be ministered unto, but to minister, and to give his life a ransom for many" (Matthew 20:28). The importance of Christ's death is seen in that it forms the heart of the gospel. Paul wrote, "I declare unto you the gospel which I preached unto you . . . how that Christ died for our sins according to the scriptures; And that he was buried, and that he rose again the third day according to the scriptures" (1 Corinthians 15:1, 3, 4).

Over the doors of a church in Germany there is cut in stone a beautiful lamb. The story is that a man at work on the steeple of the church lost his footing and plunged to the ground below. A flock of sheep chanced to be grazing in the churchyard, and the fall of the man was broken on a little lamb. The lamb was killed, but the man's life was saved. In his gratitude he cut into the stone over the doors of the church the lamb that saved his life.

Central to the gospel message is that the Lamb of God shed His blood that we might be forgiven and pardoned and saved from the penalty of sin.

UNDERSTANDING WHAT YOU READ

Note: *You may want to use a pencil or write your answers on another sheet of paper in case corrections must be made.*

In this section you should have gained some idea of how much space the Bible gives to the subject of Christ's death. The importance of His death to your redemption was also pointed out.

1. Two Old Testament acts that typify Christ's death are _____ and _____.

2. Two groups who showed interest in the Lord's death were the _____ and _____.

3. Jesus came into the world to pay the price of _____ for mankind.

Answers, page 179.

The Purpose of Christ's Death

Christ's death reveals sin for what it is. It is the most vicious and awful thing in God's universe. We do not want to use any expression that makes sin appear respectable. Its utterly despicable nature is revealed in that it led to the crucifixion of Christ.

The sins that led up to Calvary are quite common: self-interest in Caiaphas, fear in Pilate, impurity in Herod, anger and spite in the crowd. Sins that are ordinary attitudes seen in the world every day brought about Christ's death. These sins are so lightly condoned in the world; yet, they caused the greatest crime ever committed.

At the foot of the Cross there are no great sins and lesser sins. Encouraged to repent of his sins, a man prayed, "Lord, forgive me of my sins, which are not very great." Yet, the Bible says, "For whosoever shall keep the whole law, and yet offend in one point, he is guilty of all" (James 2:10).

Calvary reveals the true nature of sin. It also brings men to repent and find redemption. It shows that Christ settled the sin question. Paul wrote, "What the Law, weakened by the flesh, could not do God has done by sending His Son to be like sinful flesh and to be a sacrifice for sin. He condemned sin in the flesh so that we who don't follow the flesh but the Spirit will be as righteous as the Law demands" (Romans 8:3, 4, BECK).

Christ's death reveals the extent of God's love. Jesus did not die to get God to change His mind and love us. God's love is eternal and unchanging. There never was a time when God had to be persuaded to love. Calvary is God's love in action. The Cross reveals the heart of God.

God does not love us because Christ died for us, but Christ died for us because God loved us. God did not hold Jesus back from the Cross—from the agonizing death, from being made a curse for us, from being made sin for us. Paul wrote, "He that spared not his own Son, but delivered him up for us all, how shall he not with him also freely give us all things?" (Romans 8:32).

A mother, in one of those special moments that make mothers what they are, drew her two-year-old daughter to her and said, "Oh, I love you!" The little girl, occupied with something else, drew away and said, "Yes, I know." Love was taken for granted.

The voice of God speaks from Calvary and says, "My child, I love you." Let's never be guilty of taking that love for granted. The windows of heaven are opened when we can learn to feel deeply. "We love him, because he first loved us" (1 John 4:19).

Christ's death reveals the only means of redemption. The writer of Hebrews said, "So Christ was once offered to bear the sins of many; and unto them that look for him shall he appear the second time without sin unto salvation" (Hebrews 9:28). Of Jesus John wrote, "Unto him that loved us, and washed us from our sins in his own blood, and hath made us kings and priests unto God and his Father; to him be glory and dominion for ever and ever. Amen" (Revelation 1:5, 6).

What a picture T. DeWitt Talmage paints: "The blood must be poured from royal arteries. But where is the King? I see many thrones and a great many occupants, yet none seem to be coming down to the rescue.

"But—after awhile—the clock in Bethlehem strikes twelve, and the silver pendulum of a star swings across the sky; I see the King of heaven rising up; and He descends! And He steps down from star to star, and from cloud to cloud, lower and lower, until He touches the sheep-covered hills, and then to another hill like a skull, bearing His cross with Him; and there at the sharp stroke of persecution, a rill, red and holy, rushes down—and we who could not be redeemed by money are redeemed by precious and imperial blood."

UNDERSTANDING WHAT YOU READ

In this section you should have learned why it was necessary for Jesus to die and the purpose behind His death.

1. _____ is the most vicious and awful thing in God's universe.

2. _____ reveals the true nature of sin.

3. God's _____ is eternal and unchanging.

4. Christ's death reveals the only _____of redemption.

Answers, page 179.

The Nature of Christ's Death

The death of Jesus was voluntary. He stated that it was within His power to be delivered from this dreadful experience if He wished (John 10:17, 18; Matthew 26:53). When Peter sought to defend Jesus in the Garden of Gethsemane, Jesus said to him, "Do you think I cannot call on my Father, and he will at once put at my disposal more than twelve legions of angels? But how then would the Scriptures be fulfilled that say it must happen in this way?" (Matthew 26:53, 54, *NIV*).

When the time came, the Lord consistently refused to be rescued from death. On one occasion when Jesus was gushing forth the emotions of His inner being, He said, "Now is my soul troubled; and what shall I say? Father, save me from this hour; but for this cause came I unto this hour" (John 12:27).

In the eternal ages past, God planned this means of redemption out of love for man. What was planned by the Holy Trinity in perfect unity Jesus carried out voluntarily. He said, "The reason my Father loves me is that I lay down my life—only to take it up again. No one takes it from me, but I lay it down of my own accord. I have authority to lay it down and authority to take it up again" (John 10:17, 18, *NIV*).

The death of Jesus was costly. The Gospel of Luke records the beautiful story of the Good Shepherd who goes out to search for the lost sheep (Chapter 15). Our attention usually focuses on the Shepherd as He returns with the injured sheep across His shoulder. But what is seldom seen is the appearance of the Shepherd when He found the sheep. At that point, the Shepherd's body was bruised and bleeding.

But none of the ransomed ever knew

How deep were the waters crossed;

Nor how dark was the night

That the Lord passed through

Ere He found His sheep that was lost!

—Elizabeth C. Clephane

At Calvary all of man's collected sins fell on Christ. He took on "the humanly impossible task, of suffering an infinite burden of penalty in a finite period of time" (Anonymous). He suffered the everlasting punishment for the guilt of all sinners in the short period of the Cross. Just as justice called upon them to suffer to the infinite lengths of eternity, it demanded that He must suffer in the infinite depths of agony. He paid that price, not for Himself, but for each of us individually and personally.

The death of Jesus was necessary. The holiness of God

demanded a sacrifice for sin. Habakkuk wrote, "Your eyes are too pure to look on evil; you cannot tolerate wrong" (Habakkuk 1:13, *NIV*). Trench commented, "When God chose that costliest means of our deliverance, sending His own Son in the likeness of sinful flesh, and for sin, we may be quite sure that at no lower price would our redemption have been possible. Nothing short of this could have satisfied the righteousness of His, which He was bound to maintain."

Jesus spoke of the necessity of His death. "As Moses lifted up the serpent in the wilderness, even so must the Son of Man be lifted up, that whoever believes in Him should not perish but have eternal life" (John 3:14, 15, *NKJV*). After His resurrection, Jesus reminded His friends that His suffering had been necessary (Luke 24.26). The angels at the tomb spoke to the bewildered women about Jesus' own words as to how He must be crucified (Luke 24:6, 7). On numerous occasions the Lord made this absolutely clear (Matthew 16:21; Luke 9:22; 17:25).

UNDERSTANDING WHAT YOU READ

In this section you should have discovered that the death of Christ was voluntary and costly, but necessary.

1. Of His life Jesus said, "No one _____ it from me, but I lay it down of my own _____."

2. Jesus grappled with "the humanly impossible task of suffering an _____ burden of penalty in a _____ period of time."

3. The _____ of God demanded a sacrifice for sin.

4. After His resurrection Jesus reminded His friends that His suffering had been _____.

Answers, page 179.

The Scope of Christ's Death

The death of Christ in its scope is both universal
and limited. It is universal in the sense that it is sufficient for all. Any man anywhere who will repent of his
sins and believe on the Lord Jesus Christ will find forgiveness and peace. This provision is not dependent
upon one's social or financial standing, background,
experience, education, race, color, or creed. It is available to anyone who will accept its conditions.

Yet, salvation is limited only to those who accept it.
It is not enough to know that the provision has been
made; a person must claim that atoning work for himself. Otherwise, as far as that individual is concerned,
Christ's sacrifice was made in vain.

During President Andrew Jackson's administration,
George Wilson was sentenced to be hanged for mail
robbery and murder. President Jackson wrote out a
pardon for Wilson. The condemned man refused it,
saying, "If I refuse the pardon; it is not a pardon."

The Attorney General, the President, and many others were confused, unable to decide whether the
President's pardon was really a pardon if George
Wilson refused it. The Supreme Court of the United
States was asked to decide the question. The Court
rendered this decision—read by Chief Justice John
Marshall: "A pardon is a paper, the value of which
depends upon its acceptance by the person implicated.
It is hardly to be supposed that one under sentence of
death would refuse to accept a pardon. But if it is
refused, it is no pardon. George Wilson must hang."

And George Wilson was hanged.

God has provided in the death of Christ the pardon
for our sins, a pardon that will be good for all eternity;

but we must accept it. John wrote, "As many as received him, to them gave he power to become the sons of God, even to them that believe on his name" (John 1:12). Peter added, "Neither is there salvation in any other: for there is none other name under heaven given among men, whereby we must be saved" (Acts 4:12).

The simplest child may accept Christ by faith, taste His goodness and mercy, and thus know Him. We do not have to know everything there is to know about theology to find Christ; we can discover Him when our heart is ready to receive Him.

Two men may sit at a table filled with delicious food, the one a doctor of chemistry with cancer of the stomach, the other an ignorant laborer with a healthy appetite. The chemical expert may take the food into the laboratoy, analyze it, and give a description of its ingredients and their nutritional value, but he cannot eat of it. The hungry laborer may know little about the chemical makeup of food, but he savors its taste, eats and digests it, and thus knows its power of nutrition by experience.

Likewise, we can know Christ, not of a head knowledge alone, but of a heart experience. And there is a difference !

UNDERSTANDING WHAT YOU READ

In this section you should have learned that Christ's death was for you personally, but that you must appropriate it to yourself.

1. The death of Christ in its scope is both
_____ and _____.

2. Jesus' death is _____ in the sense that it must be _____.

3. Even the simplest _____ may accept Christ by faith.

Answers, page 179.

FOR FURTHER STUDY

Bowdle, Donald N. *Redemption Accomplished and Applied.* Cleveland, TN: Pathway, 1972.

SELF-CHECK TEST

Read the following Scripture verses. Then, apply each verse to your life by writing a sentence beginning with the words, "This means that I...." Complete the sentence by indicating what the verses say to you personally.

1. 1 Peter 1:18, 19 _____

_____

_____

_____

2. James 2:10 _____

_____

_____

_____

3. Romans 8:32 _____

_____

_____

_____

4. Hebrews 9:28 _____

_____

_____

_____

5. John 3:14, 15 _____

_____

_____

_____

When you have finished this exercise, go on to Chapter 4.

4

REPENTANCE: A CHANGE OF HEART

When John the Baptist appeared on the New Testament scene, he was thundering forth the need for repentance. "In those days John the Baptist came, preaching in the Desert of Judea and saying, 'Repent, for the kingdom of heaven is near'" (Matthew 3:1, 2, *NIV*).

Jesus began and ended His earthly ministry emphasizing this theme. "From that time on Jesus began to preach, 'Repent, for the kingdom of heaven is near'" (Matthew 4:17, *NIV*).

"Then he opened their minds so they could understand the Scriptures. He told them, 'This is what is written: The Christ will suffer and rise from the dead on the third day, and repentance and forgiveness of sins will be preached in his name to all nations, beginning at Jerusalem'" (Luke 24:45-47, *NIV*).

God yearns for men to repent and exercises great patience toward men to encourage them to turn to Him. "The Lord is not slow in keeping his promise, as some understand slowness. He is patient with you, not wanting anyone to perish, but everyone to come to repentance" (2 Peter 3:9, *NIV*).

The Bible clearly states that unless men repent they will perish (Luke 13:3). Has the need for repentance lessened today? How do you define an act of such importance? What is repentance? The New Testament term for *repentance* means "a change of mind." However, biblical repentance has a much wider range, although it includes this element. To understand what repentance means, we must look at the Old Testament idea. There *repentance* meant "turning, or returning, to God." On numerous occasions the prophets called upon Israel to stop their rebellion against God and to turn back to Him. Israel was to give wholehearted obedience to the Lord. On this evidence we may say that *repentance* is "a sincere and thorough change of the mind and attitude toward sin." It involves a sense of personal guilt and helplessness, an awareness of dependence upon God's mercy, and a strong desire to be saved from sin.

The Confession of Sin

Confession of wrong must be made to God. All sin is committed against God, against His nature, His will, His authority, His law, His justice, His goodness. David recognized this. After his sin with Bathsheba and against her husband, he admitted that he had offended

God. The Prophet Nathan came to David and pointed out his sin to him. Then the king prayed, "Have mercy on me, O God, . . . For I know my transgressions, and my sin is always before me. Against you, you only, have I sinned and done what is evil in your sight, so that you are proved right when you speak and justified when you judge" (Psalm 51:1, 3, 4, *NIV*).

In an earlier psalm, David had wrestled with the problem of not confessing his sin and then expressed the relief of sins forgiven. "When I kept silent, my bones wasted away through my groaning all day long. For day and night your hand was heavy upon me; my strength was sapped as in the heat of summer. Then I acknowledged my sin to you and did not cover up my iniquity. I said, 'I will confess my transgressions to the Lord'—and you forgave the guilt of my sin" (Psalm 32:3-5, *NIV*).

When a person realizes that his sin is sin against God, he takes the position of the publican rather than the Pharisee (Luke 18). Jesus met on one occasion with a group of people who trusted in their own righteousness. They felt superior to others and looked down on everybody else. So He told them a parable about two men who went up to the Temple to pray. One of them was a Pharisee; the other, a publican or tax collector. The Pharisee was prideful in his prayer, a prayer that centered around himself. He declared himself to be in a class all to himself—he was not like other men. He thought of others as being robbers, evildoers, and adulterers. He was especially thankful that he was not like this tax collector. He boasted of how he fasted twice a week and gave a tenth of all he received. He confessed no sin, no wrong against God whatsoever.

But what about the publican? Did he boast of his good deeds? Did he compare himself with others? No. Conscious that he had sinned against God, he would not even look up to heaven. Instead, he beat his breast and cried, "God be merciful to me a sinner" (v. 13). Whose attitude was acceptable to God? Obviously, the man who admitted his sin and sought God's mercy.

What is your attitude toward sin? Do you think of it lightly, or do you recognize that it breaks the heart of God? Do you try to find ways to justify your conduct, or do you know that you have sinned against God? Have you confessed your sin and obtained His forgiveness?

Also, confession of wrong must be made to man. Insofar as man has been wronged by our sin, we must make confession to man. The confession should be as public as the wrong which was done. If a person's reputation has been ruined, the confession should be open and public enough to correct that situation. Every means possible should be used to right the wrong that has been done. Restitution must follow repentance.

Restitution is a lost art, it seems, but it could well be an important step on the road to peace. F. B. Meyer told of a revival meeting that was dragging along without any signs of success. Then one evening an elder arose and said, "Pastor, I don't believe there is going to be a move of God as long as Brother Jones and I won't speak to each other."

He went over to Jones and said, "Brother Jones, we have not spoken in five years. Let's bury the hatchet."

A sob broke out from the audience. Another elder arose and said, "Pastor, I've been saying mean things about you behind your back and nice things to your face. I want you to forgive me." Many arose and confessed their wrongs, and God began to visit them. A revival swept over that community for three years.

In similar fashion, the man who repents of his sin against God must also make things right with his fellowman.

UNDERSTANDING WHAT YOU READ

In this section you should have discovered that confession of sin is an essential part of repentance. You should also see that confession must be made to God and man.

1. All sin is committed against _____.
2. In the parable of two men, one of them was a _____; the other a _____.
3. Sin should not be regarded _____ , because it _____ the heart of God.
4. _____ is a lost art, it seems, but it could well be an important step on the road to peace.

Answers, page 179.

The Forsaking of Sin

True repentance produces true sorrow for sin. There is a sorrow that is faulty, because it is not toward God. Such sorrow may come from a sense of shame. The sin of the person is exposed, and he is ashamed because he has dishonored himself.

Such sorrow may be expressed because the individual faces the painful consequences of sin. He has been a gambler or a spendthrift and his money is gone; now he is sorry that he has played the fool. Or such sorrow may come when the person views the horror of the future punishment of sin. If he could be assured that no punishment would follow, he would continue in sin.

It is true that some men are aroused by fear of the wrath to come and do truly repent. But true repentance involves sorrow for the sin itself. It dreads not only the death that is the wages of sin (Romans 6:23), but also the sin that earns the wages.

The sorrow for sin that God recognizes is the sorrow that looks toward God. When the prodigal son decided to return home, he did not say, "I will arise, and go to my brother; for I have hurt my brother by leaving him to serve alone." Neither did he say, "I will arise, and go to the servants, for they were very kind to me. They are brokenhearted at my conduct." No, He said, "I will arise and go to my father, and will say unto him, Father, I have sinned against heaven, and before thee, And am no more worthy to be called thy son" (Luke 15:18, 19).

Paul referred to this genuine regret for sin against God as *godly sorrow.* "Yet now I am happy, not because you were made sorry, but because your sorrow led you to repentance. For you became sorrowful as God intended and so were not harmed in any way by us. Godly sorrow brings repentance that leads to salvation and leaves no regret, but worldly sorrow brings death" (2 Corinthians 7:9, 10, *NIV*).

Godly sorrow is sorrow that has come to see sin for what it is. "True repentance hates the sin, and not merely the penalty; and it hates the sin most of all because it has discovered and felt God's love" (William Taylor).

True repentance not only confesses and feels sorrow for sin, it also forsakes sin. "To do it no more is the truest repentance" (Martin Luther). When repentance is genuine, men turn from darkness to light and from the power of Satan unto God. These are but outward expressions of the inward act of repentance.

Isaiah wrote, "Let the wicked forsake his way and the evil man his thoughts. Let him turn to the Lord, and he will have mercy on him, and to our God, for he will freely pardon" (55:7, *NIV*). Godly sorrow determines never to sin again; that is true repentance.

Gipsy Smith gave this graphic picture of repentance: " Repentance is turning *from* sin *to* God. That is repentance —'From' 'To.' It is putting your hand on your heart and getting hold of the thing that has been your curse, the enslaving passion, the captivity, the predominating force in your existence, the blackening thing, the hellish thing, the damning thing of your soul and dragging it out—by the hair of the head and saying, 'There Lord Jesus, that is it, and I will die before I commit it again. I turn from it now, and forever.'"

Politely admitting that we have done wrong may be fashionable, but there is no repentance in it. There must be a definite break with sin. Solomon wrote, "He who conceals his sins does not prosper, but whoever confesses and renounces them finds mercy" (Proverbs 28:13, *NIV*).

In England the manager of a concert hall received a postal money order for 21 cents—conscience money from a patron who said he sneaked in without paying 30 years ago.

Can you imagine the moments of regret and remorse this patron must have had over all those years? That is the result of concealing sin. Can you imagine the relief he has experienced because he confessed his wrong and did what he could to correct it?

When a person sees sin through the crimson lens of

Calvary's cross, he has no problem in giving it up. He realizes that it is suicide to continue in it. He sees its destructive power and wants nothing more to do with it. He views it as a prison whose bars and walls hold him captive and he seeks to be free of its chains. Thus, he renounces it.

UNDERSTANDING WHAT YOU READ

In this section you should have discovered that God requires more than the confession of sins. He expects men to forsake sin also.

1. True repentance produces true _____ for sin.

2. A godly sorrow is sorrow that has come to see _____ for what it is.

3. Repentance is _____ *from* sin *to* God.

4. When a person sees sin through the crimson lens of the _____ , he has no problem in forsaking it.

Answers, page 179.

Turning to God

It is not enough to turn from sin; we must turn to God. When the Apostle Paul received his commission from the Lord to go to the Gentiles, he was told, "I am sending you to open their eyes and turn them from darkness to light, and from the power of Satan to God, so that they may receive forgiveness of sins and a place among those who are sanctified by faith in me" (Acts 26:17, 18, *NIV*). Of the Thessalonians Paul wrote: "They tell how you turned to God from idols to serve the living and true God" (1 Thessalonians 1:9, *NIV*). In each of these instances, the persons involved not only turned from their sins, but also turned to God.

Every man reaches that point where he must decide if he will turn away from his wrong and make his surrender to God. In one of his sermons, Dr. Clarence Edward Macartney referred to it as the tenth hour. The purpose of the sermon was to show how there are turning points in a man's life, and how what we do, or say, or will, or accept, or refuse, influences our life ever after. At the conclusion of the sermon he said, "This may be a tenth hour for some life. Let that bring a solemn earnestness into our preaching and praying. What an awesome thought that we speak now to some soul whose tenth hour is now beginning to strike."

The next week Macartney received a letter that told of a dark struggle, a great fear, and the joy of deliverance. The person was made to drink as bitter a cup as was ever pressed to human lips. It was a trial involving disappointment, the surrender of what was most precious, and terrible pain. The letter was also one of gratitude, the best salary of any minister. It told how that person turned away from the old life and turned to God for new life. Words of thanksgiving gushed forth as the individual told how God received him and brought peace into his life.

When the soul turns to God, it finds life. The Lord invites every person to come and to receive this beautiful gift from Him. Through Isaiah He said, "Come, all you who are thirsty, come to the waters; and you who have no money, come, buy and eat! Come, buy wine and milk without money and without cost. Why spend money on what is not bread, and your labor on what does not satisfy? Listen, listen to me, and eat what is good, and your soul will delight in the richest of fare. Give ear and come to me; hear me, that your soul may live" (55:1-3, NIV).

What happens when a man turns to God? How does heaven react? Did you know that when a sinner repents, all heaven rejoices? The angels of God are glad, and the heart of God is made happy. When Jesus told the Parable of the Lost Sheep, He added, "There will be more rejoicing in heaven over one sinner who repents than over ninety-nine righteous persons who do not need to repent. . . . There is rejoicing in the presence of the angels of God over one sinner who repents" (Luke 15:7, 10, NIV).

Do you want to get the attention of heaven? Then bring a sinner to Christ, and heaven will share in the thrill of a newborn soul. This must be the supreme result of repentance.

When a man repents, he becomes qualified to receive forgiveness and pardon. To those who were present on the Day of Pentecost Peter said, "Repent and be baptized, every one of you, in the name of Jesus Christ for the forgiveness of your sins" (Acts 2:38, NIV).

You cannot visit Baalbek in northeast Lebanon, site of the ruins of ancient Heliopolis, without recalling Hood's story "Paradise and the Peri." The peri, a fallen angel, had been promised that she could get back into paradise if she brought to the gates of heaven that which was most precious to God. All over the world she searched for that treasure. She brought first the last drop of blood from a dying patriot's heart and then a maiden's kiss of sacrificial love implanted on the brow of her dying lover. But the gates of heaven opened not. Her gifts were refused.

Then, near the ruins of Baalbek, she saw a child kneeling in prayer by a fountain. As the child was praying, a man rode up on a horse and dismounted to quench his thirst at the fountain. In his face she could see all manner of evil. But as the man stooped to lift the water to his lips, he saw the child kneeling in prayer. In a flash his hard face softened and changed, and a tear flowed down his cheek, for he recalled the day when he too was as innocent as the child and prayed for himself as the child was now praying. It was that tear of repentance that opened the gates of paradise to the lost spirit.

The heart of God is touched by the broken heart of man. The psalmist wrote, "The Lord is close to the brokenhearted and saves those who are crushed in spirit" (Psalm 34:18, *NIV*). Isaiah added, "For this is what the high and lofty One says—he who lives forever, whose name is holy: 'I live in a high and holy place, but also with him who is contrite and lowly in spirit, to revive the spirit of the lowly and to revive the heart of the contrite'" (57:15, *NIV*).

UNDERSTANDING WHAT YOU READ

In this section you should have discovered that there are two sides to repentance. You must turn not only from sin, but to God.

1. "There is _____ in the presence of the angels of God over one sinner who repents."

2. When a man repents, he becomes qualified to receive _____ and _____.

3. The heart of God is touched by the _____ of man.

Answers, page 179.

Sin is enough to break the heart and crush the spirit. It is enough to bring its victim low. Only the mercy of

God can lift the man who is stooped beneath the weight of his sin. God is ready to help every person who will renounce sin and turn to Him in faith. He is more eager to help and heal than we are to have Him do so.

> 'Tis not enough to say,
> "I'm sorry and repent"
> And then go on from day to day,
> Just as I always went.
> Repentance is to leave
> The sins we loved before,
> And show that we in earnest grieve
> By doing them no more.
>
> —Selected

FOR FURTHER STUDY

Ironside, H. A. *Except Ye Repent*. Grand Rapids, MI: Zondervan, 1937.

SELF-CHECK TEST

After you have read Chapter 4 and looked up the verses in the Bible, you should take this brief self-check test. Answer the questions without referring back to the text.

Give location only.

1. List four scriptures that show the importance of repentance:

   _____

   _____

2. List two scriptures that declare confession for wrong must be made to God:

_____

_____

3. List three scriptures that call for men to forsake sin:

_____

_____

_____

4. List three scriptures that urge men to turn to God for forgiveness:

_____

_____

_____

_____

5. List two scriptures that show what happens to a man when he repents.

_____

_____

_____

_____

When you have listed these 14 possible answers, look up the correct responses in the back of the book. If you got at least 11 answers right, you may proceed to Chapter 5. If you had four or more wrong answers, you should read this lesson again, retake the test, and then go ahead to Chapter 5.

5

FAITH:
A CHANGE OF TRUST

Repentance and faith cannot be separated. True repentance could not exist without faith. Paul said to the Ephesians, "I have declared to both Jews and Greeks that they must turn to God in repentance and have faith in our Lord Jesus" (Acts 20:21, *NIV*). He knew that wherever there is true faith, there is true repentance. They are different aspects of the same act of turning. In repentance a person turns from sin to God; in faith he turns to Christ.

The Importance of Faith

Faith is first in Paul's trinity of graces. "And now these three remain: faith, hope and love. But the greatest of these is love" (1 Corinthians 13:13, *NIV*). Although love is the greatest, faith is the first and makes possible the others.

Faith is the foundation of the spiritual temple described by the Apostle Peter. It is the element that all other Christian graces build upon. So Peter wrote: "For this very reason, make every effort to add to your faith, goodness; and to goodness, knowledge; and to knowledge, self-control; and to self-control, perseverance; and to perseverance, godliness; and to godliness, brotherly kindness; and to brotherly kindness, love" (2 Peter 1:5-7, *NIV*).

Faith is important in the mind of God. It is essential to a right relationship with Him. The writer of Hebrews declared, "Without faith it is impossible to please God, because anyone who comes to him must believe that he exists and that he rewards those who earnestly seek him" (Hebrews 11:6, *NIV*). There can be no dealings with the Almighty God unless there is absolute faith in His existence.

Jesus announced to His disciples that He was going to send the Holy Spirit to them (John 16:7-11). He said that the Spirit would be a Counselor and that He would convict the world of guilt in regard to sin and righteousness and judgment. What did He name as sin? Their unbelief (v. 9). The Spirit spoke of their failure to believe in Jesus. He did not speak of adultery, or murder, or lying, or any other serious wrong, but of lack of faith.

When Jesus visited Nazareth, He could not do any miracles there, except to heal a few sick people (Mark 6:1-6). Why? Did He have less power there than somewhere else? Was He less willing to minister to needs there than elsewhere? No! The demonstration of His power was limited by their unbelief. He was amazed at their lack of faith. Faith is important to God.

Faith is the road on which man is saved from doom

and on which he finds his highest destiny. Jesus said, "Whoever believes in the Son has eternal life, but whoever rejects the Son will not see life, for God's wrath remains on him" (John 3:36, *NIV*). Faith enables a man to obtain salvation, which rescues him from eternal separation from God and lifts him to the most noble life.

Traveling by ship in Norway, you sail slowly through the beautiful and silent fjords. You see the grand mountains rising all around and beautiful waterfalls make sweet music as they hurry down the steep cliffs on their way back to their mother, the sea. Standing on the deck of the vessel, you see the channel in front narrowing until it looks like a dead end. You seem to be sailing straight into the mountain. A few hundred yards farther and you are sure the front of the ship will strike on the iron cliffs. But just when progress seems impossible, the channel opens up and the steamer glides out upon another fjord of entrancing beauty.

So it is with the iron gates we encounter on the pilgrimage of life. Faith swings the gates open, and we pass out into the beautiful life God has provided in Christ Jesus our Lord. As we start the journey by faith, so we continue by faith and gain ultimate triumph by faith. By faith our travels end as did Pilgrim's in John Bunyan's book, *Pilgrim's Progress*, which comes to a close with these words as the weary but faithful Pilgrim safely crosses the river: "So he passed over, and all the trumpets sounded for him on the other side."

Faith is essential in Christian service. The Christian life is a faith life. Only through faith can we be a constant blessing to others or will we make an effort in behalf of others. And helping others is what Christianity is all about. Surely, these factors show how important faith is!

UNDERSTANDING WHAT YOU READ

In this section you should have discovered that faith is essential to obtaining and maintaining salvation. The Bible puts great emphasis on its importance.

1. Faith is _____ in Paul's trinity of graces.

2. Faith is essential to a _____ relationship with God.

3.In Nazareth Jesus was amazed at the people's _____ of faith.

4. Faith enables a man to _____ God's salvation.

Answers, page 180.

The Definition of Faith

Faith is one of the main themes of the Bible. It is involved in all stages of the development of biblical salvation. The attitude of faith is so much a part that the New Testament Christians are called *believers*. "All the believers were together and had everything in common" (Acts 2:44, *NIV*). So, what is faith? Is it blind belief? Does it leave out evidence or rational thought?

First, faith involves a personal relationship with God. It includes both a belief in God and believing God. When we believe in God, we fix our attention upon who He is, upon His person, upon Himself, and we trust Him. When we believe God, we trust His Word; we take Him at His Word. Faith is not belief without evidence. It is belief on the best of evidence—the word of Him who cannot lie (Titus 1:2). The writer of Hebrews stated, "Now faith is being sure of what we hope for and certain of what we do not see" (Hebrews 11:1, *NIV*).

Faith in God and His Word enabled Paul to be a calming influence in the midst of a furious storm. He had advised those responsible for the ship not to sail, but they ignored his warning. They had not been sailing long when a hurricane swept down upon them. The storm became so severe that they threw the cargo overboard. Then they tossed the ship's tackle overboard. Finally, they gave up all hope of being saved from the savage wind. At this bleakest moment, Paul stood up and told them to keep their courage. He assured them that they would be spared. He said that an angel of God had brought this good news to him. He confessed to them that he believed in God, and he believed that God would do exactly what He had said. (Read Acts 27.)

That kind of faith honors God, and God honors that kind of faith. The rest of the story is that everyone on board reached land in safety.

Second, faith involves a personal relationship with Jesus Christ. It begins with a knowledge of the claims of Christ. Paul asked, "How, then, can they call on the one they have not believed in? And how can they believe in the one of whom they have not heard? And how can they hear without someone preaching to them? And how can they preach unless they are sent? As it is written, 'How beautiful are the feet of those who bring good news!'" (Romans 10:14, 15, *NIV*).

"So, then, faith cometh by hearing . . . the word of God" (Romans 10:17). Hearing about Christ must be followed by receiving Christ. It is not enough to accept the witness God gave concerning His Son. The Son of God Himself must be received. John wrote, "And this is the testimony: God has given us eternal life, and this life is in his Son. He who has the Son has life; he who does not have the Son of God does not have life" (1 John 5:11, 12).

"At every pier along the new embankment of the

Thames," wrote Anderson, "there hangs a chain that
reaches to the water's edge at its lowest ebb. But for this,
some poor creature, struggling with death, might drown
with his very hand upon the pier. An appeal to perish-
ing sinners to trust in Christ is like calling on a drown-
ing wretch to climb the embankment wall. The glad tid-
ings, the testimony of God concerning Christ, is the
chain let down for the hand of faith to grasp. Once rescued, it is not the chain the river waif would trust for
safety, but the rock immovable beneath his feet; yet, but
for the chain, the rock might have only mocked his
struggles. And it is not the gospel message the ransomed sinner trusts in, but the living Christ of whom
the Gospel speaks; but yet it was the message that his
faith at first laid hold upon, and by it he gained an eternal standing ground upon the Rock of Ages."

Faith in Jesus Christ is relying upon Him, confident
that He will do what He promises (Hebrews 10:23, 35,
36). Salvation results from that kind of faith.

UNDERSTANDING WHAT YOU READ

In this section you should have discovered the meaning of
faith. Faith is directly tied to one's relationship with God and
with His Son, Jesus.

1. When we believe God, we trust His _____.

2. In the storm _____ believed that God
   would do exactly what He had said.

3 Faith begins with a _____ of the claims of
   Christ.

4. "It is not the gospel message the ransomed sinner trusts
   in, but the living _____ of whom the gospel
   speaks."

Answers, page 180.

The Source of Faith

Is faith a human activity or a gift from God? We must take human freedom and divine election into account. Men are free to believe, but only because the grace and power of God constrain them. Faith has both divine and human aspects.

On the divine side, faith is a gift of the Father's grace. Paul wrote, "Do not think of yourself more highly than you ought, but rather think of yourself with sober judgment, in accordance with the measure of faith God has given you" (Romans 12:3, *NIV*).

Jesus is described as "the author and perfecter of our faith" (Hebrews 12:2, *NIV*). The apostles asked the Lord to "increase our faith" (Luke 17:5, *NIV*). When the disciples were caught in a storm on the Sea of Galilee, Jesus came to them walking on the water (Matthew 14:22-33). Peter called to Him and said, "Lord, if it be thou, bid me come unto thee on the water" (v. 28). Jesus bade him come. Then Peter got out of the boat and walked on the water to Him. But the furious nature of the wind caught Peter's attention, and he took his eyes off Jesus. When he did, he began to sink, and cried out, "Lord, save me" (v. 30). As long as he was looking to Jesus, his faith was strong; as soon as he took his eyes off Jesus, his faith failed.

The Holy Spirit is the energizing source. Faith is one of the spiritual gifts He gives. "There are different kinds of gifts, but the same Spirit.... Now to each one the manifestation of the Spirit is given for the common good. To one there is given through the Spirit the message of wisdom ... to another faith by the same Spirit" (1 Corinthians 12:4, 7-9, *NIV*).

On the human side, the Word of God, prayer, and exercise of faith are involved. The Word of God is instrumental in producing faith. Paul wrote, "Faith comes from hearing the message, and the message is heard through the word of Christ" (Romans 10:17, *NIV*). There are many accounts of how the Word alone has produced faith and changed lives—stories like the one of the New York gangster who had been recently released from prison. He was on his way to join his old gang with an idea for another burglary when he stopped to pick a man's pocket on Fifth Avenue. He slipped into Central Park to see what he had stolen. He found himself in possession of a New Testament— no doubt to his deep disappointment. He had time before his meeting, so idly he began to read it, and soon he was deep into the Book. A few hours later he went to meet his comrades. He told them what he had been reading, and then once and for all he broke away from them and gave up crime. The Word of God produced a faith in his heart that changed his life and made him a new creature.

Prayer is also instrumental in producing faith. When Jesus was about to deliver a boy from a deaf and dumb spirit, He told the boy's father that if he could believe, all things were possible. The father replied, "I do believe; help me overcome my unbelief!" (Mark 9:24, *NIV*). Jesus said of Simon Peter that Satan had asked to sift him as wheat. Satan's intention was to destroy Peter. Jesus added, "But I have prayed for you, Simon, that your faith may not fail" (Luke 22:32, *NIV*).

Then, faith is developed by using what we already

have. George Mueller of Bristol, England, never claimed to have the gift of faith. He said that his faith "is the self-same faith which is found in every believer, and the growth of which I am most sensible of myself; for by little and little it has been increasing for the past sixty-nine years."

UNDERSTANDING WHAT YOU READ

In this section you should have discovered that there are two sides to the exercise of faith. Faith has both divine and human aspects.

1. Faith is a gift of the Father's _____.
2. Jesus is described as "the _____ and _____ of our faith."
3. The _____ of God is instrumental in producing faith.
4. _____ is also instrumental in producing faith.

Answers, page 180.

The Results of Faith

The Christian life is a faith life from beginning to end. Through faith we have the assurance of salvation. Paul sought to encourage Timothy by speaking of the assurance faith had brought to him. He wrote, "I know whom I have believed, and am convinced that he is able to guard what I have entrusted to him for that day" (2 Timothy 1:12, *NIV*). With this assurance comes a peace that only faith in Christ can produce. To the Romans Paul declared, "Since we have been justified through faith, we have peace with God through our Lord Jesus Christ" (5:1, *NIV*).

William Barclay wrote, "There should be in the life of a Christian a certain calm. A worried Christian is a contradiction in terms. A Christian is by definition a man who has that inner strength which enables him to cope with anything that life can do to him or bring to him. There should be in the Christian a calm, quiet, unhurried and unworried strength which is the opposite of the feverish and fretful inefficiency of the world." That serenity, that inner peace, comes through faith in Jesus Christ.

Not only is faith important to salvation, but it is essential to normal Christian development. Again, Paul wrote to the Romans, "For in the gospel a righteousness from God is revealed, a righteousness that is by faith from first to last, just as it is written: 'The righteous will live by faith'" (Romans 1:17; *NIV*). He also said, "We walk by faith, not by sight" (2 Corinthians 5:7).

Every step of our journey as a believer is accompanied by the watchful care of the Lord Jesus Christ. He pleads our case before the Father; He makes intercession for us. He loved us enough to die for us; His love continues to reach out to us. He who cared for us before we ever came to Him cares for us with a never-dying, eternal love. The Scripture says, "Therefore he is able to save completely those who come to God through him, because he always lives to intercede for them" (Hebrews 7:25, *NIV*). By faith we accept that this work of Christ is going on for us, and what a difference it makes in our life! It means the difference between defeat and victory. It is the key to our overcoming the world. "This is the victory that has overcome the world, even our faith" (1 John 5:4, *NIV*). It is also essential to our being an instrument which God can use and through whom His Spirit can flow. Jesus said, "'Whoever believes in me, as the Scripture has said, streams of living water will flow from within him.' By this he meant the Spirit, whom those who believed in him were later to receive. Up to that time the Spirit had not been given, since Jesus had not yet been glorified" (John 7:38, 39, NIV).

Through faith the believer receives the rich benefits made available by Christ at Calvary. These benefits include physical healing. A woman who had been suffering from the same sickness for 12 years came to Jesus for healing. Coming up behind Him, she touched the hem of His garment. She reasoned in her mind, "If I only touch His garment, I shall get well." That's faith! And that faith produced the response that brought her deliverance. Jesus said to her, "Your faith has made you well" (see Matthew 9:20-22, NASB). Other benefits produced by faith include answered prayer, miracle-working power, overcoming sufficiency in the daily affairs of life, and an attitude that says, "Let go and let God." Faith is up front in the achievements God works through believers.

UNDERSTANDING WHAT YOU READ

In this section you should have witnessed faith at work. Its impact is felt on the whole Christian life.

1. The Christian life is a _____ life from beginning to end.
2. Faith is essential to normal Christian _____.
3. Every step of our journey as a believer is accompanied by the _____ of the Lord Jesus Christ.

Answers, page 180.

Bancroft wrote, "By faith we lay hold of God's almightiness. Faith can do anything that God can do." What a blessed gift faith is! We ought to treasure and nurture it that it may grow and enrich our life. What we do with faith depends upon our attitude toward it. May it be stronger for our having exercised it faithfully.

FOR FURTHER STUDY

Gutzke, Manford George. *Help Thou My Unbelief.* Nashville, TN: Thomas Nelson, 1974.

SELF-CHECK TEST

After you have read Chapter 5 and looked up the verses in the Bible, you should take this brief self-check test. Answer the questions without referring back to the text.

True or False

Indicate whether each statement is True or False by writing "T" or "F" in the blank to the left.

_____ 1. True repentance never exists except in conjunction with faith.

_____ 2. Jesus never promised His disciples that He would send the Holy Spirit to them.

_____ 3. Faith is the road on which man secures his highest destiny.

_____ 4. Faith is a seldom-mentioned theme of the Bible.

_____ 5. Paul was the most frightened person on board the ship during the storm.

_____ 6. Faith comes by hearing the Word of God.

_____ 7. Faith is both a human activity and a divine gift.

_____ 8. Peter never took his eyes off of Jesus when walking on the water.

_____ 9. Inner peace comes through faith in Jesus Christ.

_____10. Christ's work in our behalf does not extend to the present day.

When you have marked the answers that you believe to be correct for these ten questions, look up the answers in the back of the book. If you got at least eight answers right, you may proceed to Chapter 6. If you had three or more wrong answers, you should read this lesson again, retake the test, and then go ahead to Chapter 6.

6

JUSTIFICATION: A CHANGE OF STANDING

ob is described as a man who was "blameless and upright; he feared God and shunned evil" (Job 1:1, NIV). The Lord Himself is said to have held this opinion of Job. How did the people view Job? This is how Job described their reaction to him: "When I went to the gate of the city and took my seat in the public square, the young men saw me and stepped aside and the old men rose to their feet; the chief men refrained from speaking and covered their mouths with their hands; the voices of the nobles were hushed, and their tongues stuck to the roof of their mouths. Whoever heard me spoke well of me, and those who saw me commended me" (Job 29:7-11, NIV).

At the height of his suffering when no one seemed to respect him, Job longed for those days when he was in his prime. How did he gain such respect? How did he earn such high esteem? He did so by righteous living which resulted in a kind and friendly relationship with his fellow man. If he knew of someone in need, he was there to lend a helping hand. He gave particular attention to orphans. His was the last face many dying people saw as he sought to bring them comfort. He employed all of his charm to bring rejoicing back to the heart of widows. Even the stranger had a friend in Job. He was "eyes to the blind and feet to the lame" (Job 29:15, *NIV*). And Job was all of this because, as he said, "I put on righteousness as my clothing; justice was my robe and my turban" (Job 29:14, *NIV*). No wonder God called Job a righteous man. No wonder that the members of his community agreed. But what makes a person righteous?

What Does Justification Mean?

In *Great Is the Lord*, Robert G. Lee illustrates justification and forgiveness. Says he, "If I am arrested under suspicion by others that I committed a crime and am hailed into court, where I declare my innocence, my lawyer calls many witnesses who testify that I was miles away when the offense was committed. My innocence is completely established. By the declaration of the judge, I leave the court without a stain upon my character. In other words, being innocent, I am completely justified.

"But if I am guilty of the offense for which I was arrested and brought into court, there are some extenuating circumstances. It is my first offense. I was drawn rather coercively into the offense against my better judgment. The judge rebukes and warns me, then discharges me. Without any penalty being inflicted. I leave the court a free man. Forgiven am I, but not cleared of the charge."

Forgiveness is one facet of justification. Man is under penalty of death because of sin. Christ suffered on Calvary to pay this penalty and to have it removed. When man repents of his sin and believes on the Lord Jesus Christ, God pardons him because Christ has borne the penalty for his sin. So Paul could write, "There is now no condemnation for those who are in Christ Jesus, . . . Who will bring any charge against those whom God has chosen? It is God who justifies. Who is he that condemns? Christ Jesus, who died—more than that, who was raised to life—is at the right hand of God and is also interceding for us" (Romans 8:1, 33, 34, *NIV*).

But justification involves more than forgiveness; it includes being restored to favor with God. Sin placed a barrier between God and man. The lines of communication were broken, and the intimate fellowship was lost. Because of sin man has placed himself under the wrath of God; but when he turns to Christ, what he lost is regained. He becomes a member of the kingdom of God with full citizenship rights. All enmity against God is gone, and the believer is a friend of God as much as Abraham was. James wrote, "'Abraham believed God, and it was credited to him as righteousness,' and he was called God's friend" (James 2:23, *NIV*; compare Genesis 15:6).

Finally, justification means having the righteousness of Christ imputed to the believer. To *impute* is to "reckon." An example is the case of Paul, Philemon, and Onesimus. (See the Epistle of Paul to Philemon.) Paul and Philemon were dear friends who worked together in the Lord's service. Onesimus had been Philemon's slave and had apparently run away without paying his debts to his master. While he was in prison, Paul met Onesimus and won him to Christ. The apostle wrote Philemon and urged him to welcome Onesimus back. He was sending him back, not as a slave, but as a dear brother. He reminded Philemon that they were partners and called on him to receive Onesimus as he would receive Paul himself. Then the apostle went a step beyond where most people would have gone. He told Philemon that if Onesimus had wronged him in any way, or if he owed him anything, he could charge that to his account. "I will pay it back," Paul assured Philemon (v. 19, *NIV*). Finally, the apostle asked Philemon to prepare a guest room for him, because he hoped to come to him in answer to prayer.

What Paul did for Onesimus, Christ did for us and more. God charged our sins to His account and imputed His righteousness to us. To the Corinthians Paul wrote, "God was reconciling the world to himself in Christ, not counting men's sins against them.... God made him who had no sin to be sin for us, so that in him we might become the righteousness of God" (2 Corinthians 5:19, 21, *NIV*).

Justification is "the act or decree of God whereby any sinner anywhere through faith in Christ is cleared of all guilt before God and declared righteous by God and looked upon by God as though that sinner had never sinned, as though he were altogether the righteousness of God" (Lee).

UNDERSTANDING WHAT YOU READ

In this section you should have discovered what it means to be justified. You should have learned what part forgiveness, restoration to favor, and the imputation of Christ's righteousness play in justification.

1. When a man is justified, he becomes a member of the kingdom of God with full _____ rights.
2. What Paul did for _____, Christ did for us and more.
3. God looks upon the justified man as though he had never _____.

Answers, page 180.

How Are Men Justified?

There are some things men practice in the hope of being justified that will not work. There are other means, however, that will result in justification.

If men are depending upon keeping the Law to justify them, they will be disappointed. The only way they could be justified by keeping the Law would be to fulfill every single aspect of the Law. No man, other than Jesus, has ever done that. As soon as one facet of the Law is broken, it becomes impossible to be justified by means of the Law. "For whoever keeps the whole law and yet stumbles at just one point is guilty of breaking all of it" (James 2:10, *NIV*).

If anyone would have expected to be justified by keeping the law, surely it would have been the rich young ruler (Luke 18). He came to Jesus and asked about obtaining eternal life. Jesus referred him to the commandments, and the young man said that he had kept all of those since he was a boy. Still, Jesus said that this was not enough. The young man was lacking in one thing. Not until he ceased trusting in things and put his trust in Jesus could he hope for eternal life. His attempts at keeping the Law could not obtain it for him.

Neither can a man be justified on the basis of good conduct. Some men seem to think that if they go to church, pay tithes, help their neighbor, and have a longer list of good deeds than bad deeds, they will be justified. The truth is that no amount of good works will justify them. While all the things mentioned are good, and every believer should practice them, they do not bring justification.

Kipling wrote a powerful poem called "Tomlinson." Tomlinson is summoned from his house in Berkeley Square and conducted by a spirit far down the Milky Way till they come to a gate in the wall, to which Peter holds the key. Peter tells Tomlinson to stand up and give an account of the good things he had done on earth.

When he hears that, the naked soul of Tomlinson grows "white as a rainwashed bone." He mentions a priest who has been his friend on earth and would answer for him if he stood by his side. But Peter tells him that he must answer for himself—that "the race is run by one and one and never by two and two." Then Tomlinson speaks of what he has read in a book—of what some man in Russia thinks—of what his own opinion or guess is. But Peter tells him that it's not what he's read, or heard, or thought, but what he has done that he is interested in. Tomlinson is then turned away from the heavenly gate.

Apparently Tomlinson does not have any good deeds to offer. But even if he had had a list as long as the Christmas list of the spoiled son of a wealthy man, it would not have been enough to secure the key that unlocks the door of justification. It cannot be done through good deeds or good conduct.

How, then, can a man be justified? First, justification comes from God and not from man. It is by the grace of God that we are justified. Paul wrote, "This righteousness from God comes through faith in Jesus Christ to all who believe. There is no difference, for all have sinned and fall short of the glory of God, and are justified freely by his grace through the redemption that came by Christ Jesus" (Romans 3:22-24, *NIV*).

In *Let Me Illustrate,* Donald Grey Barnhouse observes: "We have many examples in chemistry that show how the introduction of a second element will completely debase or transform a product. If you put a dime in a bottle of hydrogen peroxide, the silver will react so rapidly that a moment later nothing will be left in the bottle but liquid. If you put even the smallest spark of fire into a barrel of gunpowder, you will explode the whole barrel. Terrible oil refinery fires have been caused by a single drop of perchloric acid coming in contact with some heated organic liquid—gasoline, kerosene, or aniline.

"If [justification] is by grace then it is not of works, for as soon as there is a mixture of even the smallest percentage of works, grace is debased.... The whole idea of works is that man can provide a basis that will force God to give him some blessing as a just reward for the works. The whole idea of grace is that God acts toward man according to that which is to be found within his own divine nature of love." As Paul wrote, "It is by grace you have been saved" (Ephesians 2:8, *NIV*).

Second, a man is justified by the blood of Christ. In Romans 3:24 (quoted above) Paul established this fact. He was even more direct in Romans 5:9, "Since we have now been justified by his blood, how much more shall we be saved from God's wrath through him!" (*NIV*). This passage does not mean that God has excused our sins or overlooked them. What it does mean is that Jesus Christ, our substitute, was punished for them. When God raised Jesus from the dead, He testified that He was pleased with the Son's work. One author has noted, "By the resurrection, God declares that He has accepted and is satisfied with the settlement Christ has made. It shows that death to be of sufficient value to cover all our sins, for it is the sacrifice of the Son of God. My sin may be as high as the highest mountain, but the sacrifice that covers it is as high as the highest heaven. My guilt may be as deep as the ocean, but the atonement that swallows it up is as deep as eternity."

The gift of the Holy Spirit is another proof that God is pleased with the atoning death of Christ. In *Ministry of the Spirit* A. J. Gordon wrote, "Christ, our great High Priest, has entered into the Holy of Holies by His own blood. Until He comes forth again at His second advent, how can we be assured that His sacrifice for us is accepted? We could not be, unless He had sent out one from His presence to make known the fact to us. And this is precisely what He has done in the gift of the Holy Ghost."

Third, a man is justified by faith, and justification reveals itself in works. We are not justified on account of our faith as though it were some holy act or state of mind. It is not *for* faith that we are justified, but *by* faith.

JUSTIFICATION: A CHANGE OF STANDING

Faith is not the price of justification, but the acceptance of God's method of justification. It takes for oneself what grace provides. Paul said, "I want you to know that through Jesus the forgiveness of sins is proclaimed to you. Through him everyone who believes is justified from everything you could not be justified from by the law of Moses" (Acts 13:38, 39, *NIV*).

The faith that justifies leads the believer to act according to his new position in Christ. Thus being justified, he produces fruit that brings glory to God and points men to Christ. He is justified not by works, but exhibits works because he is justified. It is in this sense that James could write, "What good is it, my brothers, if a man claims to have faith but has no deeds? Can such faith save him?. . . You see that a person is justified by what he does and not by faith alone" (James 2:14, 24, *NIV*).

UNDERSTANDING WHAT YOU READ

In this section you should have learned how to be justified. You should also have seen that there are some things men trust in that will not justify them, and there are other things that will bring justification.

1. The only way men could be justified by keeping the Law would be to fulfill every single _____ of the Law.

2. Good deeds can never secure the key that unlocks the door of _____.

3. "My _____ may be as high as the highest _____ , but the _____ that covers it is as high as the highest _____."

4. It is not _____ faith that we are justified, but _____ faith.

Answers, page 180.

What Happens When Men Are Justified?

Some of the results of justification were covered in the section about its meaning. There we noted that forgiveness of sins and the removal of sin's penalty are part of being justified. Also, the justified man is restored to favor with God. In addition, Christ's righteousness is given to the believer. As Henry C. Thiessen says, "The believer is now clothed in a righteousness not his own, but provided for him by Christ, and is therefore accepted into fellowship with God."

The justified man is made an heir of God. Paul wrote, "He saved us through the washing of rebirth and renewal by the Holy Spirit, whom he poured out on us generously through Jesus Christ our Savior, so that, having been justified by his grace, we might become heirs having the hope of eternal life" (Titus 3:5-7, *NIV*).

Alfred Dreyfus was a Jewish French army officer who was arrested on suspicion of spying for Germany. A military court found him guilty and suspended him from the army. It sentenced him to life imprisonment on Devil's Island. In the presence of his own regiment, his sword was taken from him, the epaulettes were torn from his shoulders, and his uniform was stripped from him.

Dreyfus was allowed a second trial because of the influence of some friends. But this trial was a mockery. Testimony favorable to Dreyfus was not allowed. He was imprisoned again. Champions of justice throughout the world protested the unfair trial. Finally, the case was reviewed by the highest court in France, and Dreyfus was declared innocent. He was given the position in his regiment that he would have occupied if he had never been arrested. It was reckoned that if he had never left his regiment, he would have risen to the rank of colonel; therefore, he was made colonel.

Likewise, when a man is justified, he is not only forgiven and restored to favor with God, but given the position that would have been his if he had never sinned. He is declared to be a son of God. He is declared to be an heir of God and a joint heir with Jesus Christ. Paul wrote, "The Spirit himself testifies with our spirit that we are God's children. Now if we are children, then we are heirs—heirs of God and co-heirs with Christ, if indeed we share in his sufferings in order that we may also share in his glory" (Romans 8:16, 17, *NIV*).

UNDERSTANDING WHAT YOU READ

In this section you should have discovered the beautiful privileges that come to the justified man.

1. The justified man is restored to _____ with God.
2. When a man is justified, he is given the _____ that would have been his if he had never sinned.
3. He is declared to be an _____ of God and a _____ with Jesus Christ.

Answers, page 180.

The final word in justification, as in all salvation, is Jesus Christ. He forgives; He restores favor; He gives His righteousness; He makes us heirs of God. Through Him we have a relationship with God that we could never have had otherwise. He makes it possible for us to walk in newness of life. New dimensions of living are opened up to all those who know Him. He invites men to move away from a mere existence and to experience real life. The soul of man will never know lasting, permanent satisfaction until it receives new life from Christ.

FOR FURTHER STUDY

Pearlman, Myer. *Knowing the Doctrines of the Bible.*
Springfield, MO: Gospel, 1937.

SELF-CHECK TEST

After you have read Chapter 6 and looked up the verses in the Bible, you should take this brief self-check test. Answer the questions without referring back to the text.

1. List three facets of justification:

   _____

   _____

   _____

2. List two practices that will not produce justification:

   _____

   _____

3. List three things that are instrumental in a man being justified:

   _____

   _____

   _____

4. List two evidences that God is satisfied with the atoning death of Christ:

   _____

   _____

5. List four results of justification:

_____

_____

_____

_____

When you have listed these 14 possible answers, look up the correct responses in the back of the book. If you got at least 11 answers right, you may proceed to Chapter 7. If you had four or more wrong answers, you should read this lesson again, retake the test, and then go ahead to Chapter 7.

7

REGENERATION: A CHANGE OF NATURE

He had one of the sharpest minds of any man I have ever met. As a farmer/businessman, he showed unusual shrewdness. His political influence was evident because he served as a colonel (an honorary position) on the staff of two Mississippi governors. He was liked and respected by people from all spectrums of society. But K. C. Peters was not a Christian.

Usually a very confident man, at one point in his life this native of Charleston, Mississippi, became obsessed with fear about his health. He seemed utterly helpless in trying to overcome his fear. He spent some time in a hospital and eventually was given electrical shock treatments to erase from his mind the thoughts that were causing him to be afraid.

During this time, the Holy Spirit began to deal with him about his spiritual needs. Even after he had gone home from the hospital, the Spirit continued to speak to him.

One morning I felt an inner urge to go to K. C.'s house. When I arrived—his house was located in a beautiful rustic setting—he met me at the door and said: "Preacher, the Lord sent you here this morning. I've gone three times to get my hat to go to town, and for some reason I just couldn't leave." Then he added, "I want to be saved."

We went into the house, sat down on the sofa, and talked about the plan of salvation. I suggested that he needed to ask God to forgive him for the wrong he had done. He responded, "Preacher, I've asked God to forgive me of every sin that I can think of that I've ever committed. I've told Him that if I have forgotten any sin, if He will bring it to my attention, I will ask His forgiveness for that too."

I told K. C. that if he had come to grips with the sin in his life, all he needed to do now was to place his faith in Jesus Christ and invite the Savior to come into his heart. At that point, we knelt together, and K. C. prayed the sinner's prayer.

After the prayer, he looked at me as tears streamed down his cheeks and said, "Preacher, I feel something that I've never felt before. I feel clean and peaceful in my heart." Such was the character of this man that he apologized for his tears.

The Lord gloriously saved K. C. Peters that morning. He became one of the best friends I have ever had.

Though he has gone on to be with the Lord, I am still influenced by his life. His experience is just one example of the complete change that takes place when a person is regenerated.

The Need for Regeneration

> *A man said to the Universe,*
>
> *"Sir, I exist!"*
>
> *"However," replied the Universe,*
>
> *"That fact has not created in me*
>
> *A sense of obligation."*
>
> *—Stephen Crane (War is Kind)*

Modern literature, for the most part, abounds in hopelessness. It has brought to the thought of modern man many different philosophies. Each of these ideas provide little hope. Obviously, man realizes his condition, but it is also obvious that he has no solution to his dilemma. And though he search through the whole world and through his mind, no solution can be found, because there is no solution except through Christ.

Without Christ, modern literature paints an accurate picture of the human condition: a life without hope, a life where death is the end. However, the alternative, a Christ-centered life, offers life—eternal life. And the only way to obtain a Christ-centered life and eternal life is through the process of regeneration. There is no other way.

In reaching out for God, man discovers barriers that must be overcome. As already noted, man is selfish where God is holy; man is weak where God is strong;

man is evil where God is love. Man's sinful condition cannot come near the holiness of God. Sin has separated man from the life of God, so that he is "alienated from the life of God."

So how is a reunion to be brought about? Since God and man are enemies, a subjective change must take place in one or both before there can be a reconciliation. But God is unchangeable; and since man is evil, the change must take place in him. A complete turnabout must take place. Nothing short of a complete remake of man will do, and this change can be achieved only through God. We are "born, not of blood, nor of the will of the flesh, nor of the will of man, but of God" (John 1:13). Emery H. Bancroft said in *Elemental Theology*:

> *That which is in the mineral kingdom cannot of itself unaided gain entrance into the kingdom just above, the vegetable kingdom. Vegetable life must reach down into the mineral kingdom and impart itself to that which is in that domain, and thus lift it from the one to the other. The same is true of that which is in the vegetable kingdom in relation to the animal kingdom. The same principle also obtains with reference to man in the kingdom of God. Man is now in the kingdom of nature, which has become the kingdom of darkness, even Satan's kingdom, and unless he is born from above he must there forever remain. The life of God in the Holy Spirit must reach down into that kingdom and impart itself to those who are its subjects and thus translate them into the kingdom of God.*

"The heart is more deceitful than all else, and is desperately sick; Who can understand it?" (Jeremiah 17:9,

NASB). "Transgression speaks to the ungodly within his heart; There is no fear of God before his eyes" (Psalm 36:1, *NASB).* Man needs a change in nature so that he can be counted among those "that thought upon his name" (Malachi 3:16). No education or culture can bring about such a needed change; God alone can do it.

Man is essentially bad. "They that are in the flesh cannot please God" (Romans 8:8) nor "inherit the kingdom of God" (1 Corinthians 6:9, 10; 15:50). The flesh cannot be improved. "Can the Ethiopian change his skin or the leopard his spots? then may ye also do good, that are accustomed to do evil" (Jeremiah 13:23). What man needs is not to try and improve his nature, but to get a new one through the process of regeneration.

The need for regeneration is universal. No age, sex, position, or condition exempts anyone from this necessity. Not to be born again is to be lost. There is no substitute for the New Birth. "Neither circumcision availeth any thing, nor uncircumcision, but a new creature" (Galatians 6:15). Education, morality, religion, form, ritual, baptism, reform—none of these nor any combination of them are enough. "Ye must be born again" (John 3:7).

UNDERSTANDING WHAT YOU READ

1. No solution can be found for man's condition except
   _____.

2. Man's _____condition cannot come near the
   _____of God.

3. "They that are in the flesh cannot _____ God"
   nor " _____the kingdom of God."

4. Not to be born again is to be _____.

Answers, page 181.

The Meaning of Regeneration

John in his Gospel related the story of a man named Nicodemus (Chapter 3). He was a Pharisee and a member of the Jewish ruling council, a very important man in the community. One night Nicodemus came to Jesus and said, "Rabbi, we know you are a teacher who has come from God. For no one could perform the miraculous signs you are doing if God were not with him" (v. 2, *NIV*). In reply Jesus said, "I tell you the truth, no one can see the kingdom of God unless he is born again" (v. 3, *NIV*). A confusing statement indeed, and Nicodemus, unsure of what Jesus was talking about, asked, "But how can a man be born when he is old?" And, of course, Nicodemus was justified (as are we) in asking what is meant by being born again.

Henry C. Thiessen in *Lectures in Systematic Theology* defines regeneration "as the communication of divine life to the soul (John 3:5; 10:10, 28; 1 John 5:11, 12), as the impartation of a new nature (2 Peter 1:3) or heart (Jeremiah 24:7; Ezekiel 11:19; 36:26), and the production of a new creation (2 Corinthians 5:17; Ephesians 2:10; 4:24)."

Regeneration is the communication of new and divine life to the soul, a new creation, the production of a new thing. It is not the old nature fixed up or strengthened, but a New Birth from above. By nature, man is dead in sin. Through sin, man's spirit came into a condition of spiritual death. A division between God and man took place through disobedience. The New Birth imparts to man new life—the life of God—so that from now on he is alive from the dead; he has "passed from death unto life" (John 5:24). He is brought out of his spiritual death into spiritual life and communion with God.

Regeneration is the giving of a new nature of heart. The unregenerate man is blind to the Truth, "the things of the Spirit," corrupt in his desires, and perverse in his will (Romans 8). This is the condition of every unregenerate man, no matter how educated, refined, or moral he may appear. In regeneration we are made partakers of the divine nature—God's nature. God gives to us His own wise and holy nature, a nature that thinks as God thinks, feels as God feels, wills as God wills. "Old things are passed away; behold, all things are become new" (2 Corinthians 5:17).

Regeneration is the production of a new creation. Evans said, "It is not evolution, but involution—the communication of a new life. It is a revolution—a change of direction resulting from that life. It is a crisis with a view to a process. A new governing power comes into the regenerate man's life by which he is enabled to become holy in experience." The change is neither in the substance nor in the mere exercise of the soul, but in those attitudes, principles, tastes, or habits that underlie all conscious activity exercise and determine the character of the man—his "ways."

Regeneration is not reformation. It seems almost fitting that Jesus should reveal his plan of regeneration to a Pharisee. The Pharisees put great emphasis on obeying the Law, but Jesus said in essence that outward obedience is not enough. Regeneration alone can meet the need of man and the requirement of God.

Lasher said: "The Pharisees were the best people of their day, and yet they were the greatest failures. Against no others did Jesus hurl so fierce denunciations.

Why? Because they put reformation in the place of repentance and faith; because they were employing human means for accomplishing what only the Holy Spirit could accomplish. And so, today every device for the betterment of society which does not strike at the root of the disease and apply the remedy to the seat of life, the human soul, is Pharisaical and is doing a Pharisee's work."

Regeneration is not baptism. This final note is necessary because some people claim that John 3:5 ("Except a man be born of water and of the Spirit") and Titus 3:5 ("the washing of regeneration") teach that regeneration occurs in connection with baptism. But as Mullins says:

> *Regeneration is not effected through the act of baptism. In a number of New Testament passages baptism is clearly associated with conversion, and nearly always with the beginnings of the Christian life (see Acts 2:38; Romans 6:3, 4; 1 Peter 3:21). But there is no evidence that in any of these passages baptism is regarded . . . as an act which of itself regenerates without reference to the mind of the recipient. Nor do they sustain the view . . . that baptism completes the act of regeneration. The error in both views is in regarding baptism as a means to a given end, when it is only the symbolic outward expression of the end when it has otherwise been accomplished. Baptism symbolizes regeneration but it does not produce it. The true significance of baptism is moral and spiritual. It is the answer of a good conscience toward God.*

UNDERSTANDING WHAT YOU READ

1. Regeneration is the communication of _____ and _____ life to the soul.

2. Regeneration is the impartation of a _____.

3. Regeneration is the _____ of a new creation.

4. Regeneration is not _____ or _____.

Answers, page 181.

The Means of Regeneration

Everyone is probably familiar with the story of Paul and Silas in jail (Acts 16). About midnight Paul and Silas were praying and singing hymns to God when suddenly there was a violent earthquake that shook the prison doors open and shook Paul's and Silas' chains loose. The jailer woke up; and when he saw that the prison doors were open, he drew his sword and started to kill himself because he thought the prisoners had all escaped. But Paul told him that they had not escaped and told him not to harm himself. The jailer then fell down before Paul and Silas and asked, "What must I do to be saved?" (v. 30). They replied, "Believe on the Lord Jesus, and thou shalt be saved" (v. 31).

It's that simple. So simple that it's often overlooked. Although the gospel message is heard on radio stations, presented on television, sung on street corners, preached from pulpits, and explained in books and tracts, millions of people overlook it. All we have to do to be born again is to repent of our sins and believe on the Lord Jesus as our personal Lord and Savior. We don't clean up, give up, or turn around ourselves; we just come as we are.

God has provided us with a simple solution. Simple for man, that is. God's contribution is a little more involved.

We are "born, not of blood, nor of the will of the flesh, nor of the will of man, but of God" (John 1:13). Our regeneration is an act of God, not a reforming process on the part of man. It is not by natural choice, nor by self-effort, nor by any human creative process, nor by the blood of sacrifices, nor by natural inheritance. It is altogether and absolutely the work of God. Practically speaking, we have no more to do with our second birth than we had to do with our first birth, only to accept it.

Of course, the central theme of regeneration, as well as the central theme of Christianity and the whole Bible, is the death and resurrection of Christ. The New Birth is based on the crucified Christ—"Just as Moses lifted up the snake in the desert, so the Son of Man must be lifted up, that everyone who believes in him may have eternal life" (John 3:14, 15, *NIV*)—and the resurrected Christ—"In his great mercy he has given us new birth into a living hope through the resurrection of Jesus Christ from the dead" (1 Peter 1:3, *NIV*).

And the Word of God is also instrumental in the process of regeneration, as are ministers who proclaim the Word. Peter wrote, "For you have been born again . . . through the living and enduring word of God" (1 Peter 1:23 *NIV*). And Paul said that he had begotten the Corinthians through the gospel (1 Corinthians 4:15).

But the main force behind regeneration is the Holy Spirit. Truth does not in itself affect the will. The unregenerate heart hates the Truth until it is touched by the Holy Spirit.

James Strong says, "No mere increase of light can enable a blind man to see; the disease of the eye must first be cured before external objects are visible.... Although wrought in conjunction with the presentation of truth to the intellect, regeneration differs from moral [per]suasion in being an immediate act of God."

R. A. Torrey sums up the means of regeneration by saying, "In the New Birth the Word of God is the seed; the human heart is the soil; the preacher of the Word is the sower, and drops the seed into the soil; God by His Spirit opens the heart to receive the seed; the hearer believes; the Spirit quickens the seed into life in the receptive heart; the new Divine Nature springs up out of the Divine Word; the believer is born again, created anew, made alive, passed out of death into life."

UNDERSTANDING WHAT YOU READ

1. "_____ on the Lord Jesus, and thou shalt be saved."
2. Regeneration is a _____ act of God, not a _____ process on the part of man.
3. The central theme of regeneration is the _____ and _____ of Christ.
4. The real efficient agent in regeneration is_____.

Answers, page 181.

The Results of Regeneration

In Leviticus 25, God outlined two laws of kindness for the Israelites: the Sabbath year and the Year of Jubilee. Every seventh year all debts were canceled, all slaves were set free, and no one was to work the land.

Every fiftieth year, the Year of Jubilee, everything reverted to its original owner—whether land, livestock, or property.

Regeneration is similar to (1) the Year of Jubilee in that man is returned to his original owner (God) and (2) the Sabbath year in that his debts are canceled and he is set free. It differs in that there is no set time for regeneration; it is always available.

Regeneration opens the way to becoming children of God. John wrote, "Yet to all who received him, to those who believed in his name, he gave the right to become children of God" (John 1:12, *NIV*). As children of God we enjoy certain family privileges, such as the supply of our needs, a revelation of the Father's will and keeping grace.

Regeneration involves ceasing to sin and putting on holiness or righteousness as a life practice. It frees man from the slavery of the flesh. Although the regenerated man does not do the will of the flesh, he still has the flesh (see Galatians 5:16, 17).

A radical change takes place in the regenerated man's life and experience. It is not gradual, but immediate, although some of its manifestations may be gradual. His attitude changes; he habitually loves "the brethren," God, God's Word, his enemies, and lost souls.

These results may not be visible to the world, but they are nevertheless very real to the one who has been born into God's family.

UNDERSTANDING WHAT YOU READ

1. Regeneration opens the way to becoming_____ of God.
2. Regeneration involves ceasing to _____ and putting on holiness and _____ as a life practice.
3. Regeneration frees man from the sphere and slavery of the _____.
4. The regenerated man's _____ changes.

Answers, page 181.

FOR FURTHER STUDY

Graham, Billy. *How to Be Born Again*. Waco, TX: Word, 1979.

SELF-CHECK TEST

After you have read Chapter 7 and looked up the verses in the Bible, you should take this brief self-check test. Answer the questions without referring back to the text.

True or False

Indicate whether each statement is True or False by writing "T" or "F" in the blank to the left.

_____ 1. For regeneration man needs only to cultivate and improve his nature.

_____ 2. There are no exemptions to regeneration.

_____ 3. A new nature—God's nature—is imparted to the regenerated man.

_____ 4. The Pharisees were failures because they put repentance and faith in the place of reformation.

_____ 5. Baptism completes the act of regeneretion.

_____ 6. All you have to do to be born again is to repent of your sins, believe in the Lord Jesus, and turn yourself around.

_____ 7. The New Birth is conditioned on the crucified and resurrected Christ.

_____ 8. The unregenerate heart hates the Truth until wrought upon by the Holy Spirit.

_____ 9. The new nature received in regeneration destroys the old nature.

_____10. The results of regeneration are always visible to the world.

When you have marked the answers for these ten questions, look up the answers in the back of the book. If you got at least eight answers right, you may proceed to Chapter 8. If you had three or more wrong answers, you should read this lesson again and retake the test.

8

ADOPTION: A CHANGE OF FAMILY

The Apostle Paul was the only New Testament writer to develop the doctrine of adoption. He made five references to it (Romans 8:15, 23; 9:4; Galatians 4:5; and Ephesians 1:5). We shall look at his meaning in these verses as we study this subject.

Adoption has to do with sonship. The believer becomes a child of God in regeneration. In adoption he receives a place as an adult son. As William Evans expresses it, "The child becomes a son, the minor becomes an adult." So adoption may be described as a change of position.

The Meaning of Adoption

Two practices of the Greco-Roman world need to be understood as we look at the meaning of adoption. The first has to do with a child born into a family. Bancroft points out that at a certain time appointed by law, the male child in the family would be formally and legally adopted. That means that he was placed in the position of a legal son and was given all the privileges of a son.

Paul made reference to this practice when he wrote to the Galatians: "What I am saying is that as long as the heir is a child, he is no different from a slave, although he owns the whole estate. He is subject to guardians and trustees until the time set by his father.... When the time had fully come, God sent his Son, born of a woman, born under law, to redeem those under law, that we might receive the full rights of sons.... So you are no longer a slave, but a son; and since you are a son, God has made you also an heir" (Galatians 4:1-7, NIV).

The second practice has to do with one man taking another's to be his son and giving that son the same position and advantages of a son by birth; this is our concept of adoption. William Barclay lists four main consequences of this practice of adoption.

First, the adopted person lost all rights in his old family and gained all the rights of a fully legitimate son in his new family.

Second, it followed that he became heir to his new father's estate. Barclay points out that even if other sons were born afterward who were real blood relations, it did not affect his rights.

Third, in law, the old life of the adopted person was completely wiped out. He was regarded as a new person entering into a new life unaffected by the past.

Fourth, in the eyes of the law the adopted person was literally and absolutely the son of his new father.

Barclay turns to Roman history for an outstanding case of the adopted son being totally accepted into the family of his new father. The Emperor Claudius adopted Nero, so that Nero could succeed him on the throne. They were not in any way blood relations. Claudius already had a daughter, Octavia. To cement the alliance, Nero wished to marry Octavia. Even though Nero and Octavia were not actually related, in the eyes of the law they were brother and sister. Before they could be married the Roman senate had to pass special legislation to enable Nero to marry a girl who was legally his own sister (from *The Daily Study Bible: the Letter to the Romans* by William Barclay).

The case of Moses is a biblical example of adoption. Pharaoh issued an order that every boy born in a Hebrew home was to be killed. When Moses was born, his mother hid him for three months. When she could hide him no longer, she placed him in a basket and put it among the reeds along the bank of the Nile. When Pharaoh's daughter came down to the Nile to bathe, she saw the basket and told her slave girl to get it. When she opened the basket, the baby was crying, and she felt sorry for him.

Then Moses' sister, who was hiding nearby, asked Pharaoh's daughter if she wanted her to get one of the Hebrew women to nurse the child. Pharaoh's daughter told her yes, and she went and got the baby's mother. So the mother took the baby and cared for him. When the child grew older, Pharaoh's daughter took him and he became her son. As her adopted son,

Moses was entitled to all the rights and privileges that
would have been his if he had been of her own flesh
and blood. He could have exercised those rights to the
fullest if he had not chosen rather to go with the people of God. He gave up the pleasures and powers that
were legally his, because he was looking beyond the
temporary benefits of Egypt to the eternal rewards for
God's people.

Likewise, in adoption we become sons of God with
all the rights and privileges of sonship. We are
presently sons of God, and only the future will reveal
all that we shall be.

UNDERSTANDING WHAT YOU READ

In this section you should have discovered something
about the culture out of which the teaching of adoption rose.

1. Adoption means giving a son the same _____
   and _____ of his new father.
2. In the eyes of the law, the adopted person was literally
   and absolutely the _____ of his new father.
3. The case of _____ is a biblical example of
   adoption.

Answers, page 181.

The Time of Adoption

Plans and provision for our adoption were made
long ago. Paul wrote, "For he chose us in him before
the creation of the world to be holy and blameless in
his sight. In love he predestined us to be adopted as
his sons through Jesus Christ, in accordance with his
pleasure and will" (Ephesians 1:4, 5, *NIV*).

In personal experience, adoption takes place at the moment we believe on the Lord Jesus Christ. Paul declared, "You are all sons of God through faith in Christ Jesus" (Galatians 3:26, *NIV*). John also spoke of the present privilege of sonship: "Beloved, now are we the sons of God" (1 John 3:2).

Although every believer is presently a son of God, not every believer lives like a son of God. Many believers live as far below their privilege in Christ as the elder son did in the Parable of the Prodigal Son (Luke 15). When the prodigal son returned home, his father wanted to have a feast and celebrate. When the older son heard the music and dancing, he asked one of the servants what was going on. The servant told him that the father was celebrating because his son was back safe and sound.

The older son became angry and would have nothing to do with the party. His father went out to talk with him. The son complained that the father had never given a party for him and his friends. He spoke of his loyalty and faithfulness. The father reminded him that everything he had belonged to the son. The older son, he said, was always there with him, but this other son had been lost and was found. This was cause for celebration.

How do we act in light of our sonship? Do we stay out in the field with the servants and have to ask them what is happening in the Father's house? Or are we seated at the Father's table eating of the delicious food He offers and learning firsthand what He is saying and doing? Even as a son we can play the role of a slave, but we do not have to. We are sons of God, and we are entitled even now to all the privileges of sonship.

The complete realization of our sonship will not be known until the coming of Christ. Paul wrote, "Not only so, but we ourselves, who have the firstfruits of the Spirit, groan inwardly as we wait eagerly for our adoption as sons, the redemption of our bodies" (Romans 8:23, *NIV*).

William Evans suggests that "here in this world we are incognito; we are not recognized as sons of God. But some day we shall throw off this disguise."

Paul knew this and wrote, "For we must all appear before the judgment seat of Christ, that each one may receive what is due him for the things done while in the body, whether good or bad" (2 Corinthians 5:10, *NIV*).

John looked ahead to that moment of fuller realization and wrote, "Beloved, now are we the sons of God, and it doth not yet appear what we shall be: but we know that, when he shall appear, we shall be like him; for we shall see him as he is" (1 John 3:2).

Along this same line Paul wrote, "But our citizenship is in heaven. And we eagerly await a Savior from there, the Lord Jesus Christ, who, by the power that enables him to bring everything under his control, will transform our lowly bodies so that they will be like his glorious body" (Philippians 3:20, 21, *NIV*).

So, even our body will know His delivering touch and our transformation will be complete. The full working and manifestation of our adoption will be realized. May we say with John, "Lord, hasten the day."

UNDERSTANDING WHAT YOU READ

In this section you should have discovered that there is a past, a present, and a future to the timetable of adoption.

1. Plans and provision for our adoption were made _____.

2. In personal experience, adoption takes place at the _____ we believe on the Lord Jesus Christ.

3. The complete realization of our sonship will not be known until the _____ of Christ.

4. Although every believer is presently a son of God, not every believer _____ like a son of God.

Answers, page 181.

The Results of Adoption

There is a sense in which we identify with Jesus, and He with us, in sonship. The Bible says, "In bringing many sons to glory, it was fitting that God, for whom and through whom everything exists, should make the author of their salvation perfect through suffering. Both the one who makes men holy and those who are made holy are of the same family. So Jesus is not ashamed to call them brothers" (Hebrews 2:10, 11, *NIV*). Jesus is described as "the image of the invisible God" (Colossians 1:15, *NIV*), and as "the radiance of God's glory and the exact representation of his being" (Hebrews 1:3, *NIV*).

Believers have not reached that level, indeed cannot reach that level, but we "are being transformed into his likeness with ever-increasing glory, which comes from the Lord" (2 Corinthians 3:18, *NIV*). Through the work of adoption we are moving toward the fulfillment of the purpose for which we were created. The record is, "Then God said, 'Let us make man in our image, in our likeness.' . . . So God created man in his own image, in the image of God he created him; male and female he created them" (Genesis 1:26, 27, *NIV*). The complete fulfillment of that purpose will not take place until the life to come. What a glorious future awaits those who are called sons of God!

Being sons, we are members of the family of God, and receive from Him the love and care and nurture that a loving father freely bestows. On one occasion Jesus emphasized the contrast between an earthly father and the Heavenly Father. He reminded us that if we being evil do good things for our children, how much more will our Father in heaven bestow blessings upon His children (Matthew 7:9-11). If we stop and think of how much a parent loves a child and how much He is willing to do for that child, we get some idea of God's love. We are only human and at best there are limits to the reach of our love, but God's love has no limit.

God manifests His love in the way that is best for the members of the family. Sometimes He seeks to console us when we are beset by problems. Paul wrote that He "comforts us in all our troubles, so that we can comfort those in any trouble with the comfort we ourselves have received from God" (2 Corinthians 1:4, *NIV*). God manifests His love to us that we may understand what love is all about and that His love may flow from our heart to others.

There are times when God manifests His love in discipline. It is not that He wants to inflict harm upon us, but that He wishes to prevent our bringing harm to ourselves. The writer of Hebrews taught that we are not to make light of the Lord's discipline or to lose heart because of it (Hebrews 12:6-11). He assured that the Lord acts out of love and that chastening is an indication that we have been accepted as sons. In time, discipline produces a harvest of righteousness and peace.

Sonship also means that we bear the family name, the name of God. Paul wrote, "I kneel before the Father, from whom his whole family in heaven and on earth derives its name" (Ephesians 3:14, *NIV*).

In *Macartney's Illustrations*, the story is told of an Oriental king who once summoned into his presence his three sons. He set before them three sealed urns— one of gold, the other of amber, and the third of clay. The king bade his eldest son to choose among these three urns that which appeared to him to contain the greatest treasure. The eldest son chose the vessel of gold, on which was written the word *Empire*. He opened it and found it full of blood. The second chose the vase of amber, whereon was written the word *Glory*; and when he opened it, he found it full of ashes of men who had made a great name in the world. The third son chose the vessel of clay, and on the bottom of this vessel was inscribed the name of God. The wise men at the king's court voted that the third vessel weighed the most, because a single letter of the name of God weighed more than all the rest of the universe.

We who are sons of God bear that great and glorious name.

UNDERSTANDING WHAT YOU READ

In this section you should have discovered some of the benefits that come to believers when they are adopted into the family of God. The joys of sonship are numerous.

1. There is a sense in which we _____ with Jesus, and He with us, in sonship.

2. We receive from God the love and care and _____ that a loving father freely bestows.

3. Sonship also means that we bear the _____ name, the name of God.

4. Sometimes God seeks in love to _____ us; sometimes His love is manifested in _____.

Answers, page 181.

Evidences of Adoption

In adoption God gives the believer an earnest of the inheritance he is to receive in the future. An *earnest* is "a part of the price, paid down to bind a bargain." It is "anything that shows what is to come; a pledge; a token." If a couple is buying a house, we might say that they paid $2,000 earnest money on the house. With the $2,000 they are binding the owner to the deal they have made and pledging that this is only a deposit; the rest of the price is to come.

The earnest of the inheritance that God gives is the Holy Spirit Himself. Paul wrote, "And you also were included in Christ when you heard the word of truth, the gospel of your salvation. Having believed, you were marked in him with a seal, the promised Holy Spirit, who is a deposit guaranteeing our inheritance until the redemption of those who are God's possession—to the praise of his glory" (Ephesians 1:13, 14, *NIV*).

The Spirit leads us to greater conformity to the image of Christ. As we follow His guidance, our life is made richer and fuller. It takes on meaning and purpose because it is being directed by the all-wise One. To the Romans Paul wrote, "Those who are led by the Spirit of God are sons of God" (8:14, *NIV*).

In adoption, because we are sons, we gain confidence with certainty and security. We are no longer servants, we are sons; we have been made heirs. The Holy Spirit within us testifies that we are the children of God. The Spirit comes into our heart not to bring fear, but to promote confidence.

Writing to Timothy, Paul said, "God did not give us a spirit of timidity, but a spirit of power, of love and of self-discipline" (2 Timothy 1:7, *NIV*). Paul was telling Timothy what every believer needs to hear. We are not to walk through this world with head bowed and shoulders slumped. We are the children of God, and that is the highest position anyone can occupy on the earth. It is all by grace; we do not deserve it; nevertheless, God has arranged it. Realizing that we are who we are by the grace of God, we have every right to live as sons of God.

In adoption, because we are sons, we may have an audience with the Father whenever we need to approach Him. We come to Him in the name of Jesus, and through faith in our Lord, we boldly and confidently address the Father. Jesus understood our weaknesses and our needs. He has faced the same things we are facing and knows the difficulties involved. He is ready to plead our case before the Father and obtain mercy for us. He takes our imperfect prayers and perfects them.

It was with this in mind that the writer of Hebrews said, "We do not have a high priest who is unable to sympathize with our weaknesses, but we have one who has been tempted in every way, just as we are—yet was without sin. Let us then approach the throne of grace with confidence, so that we may receive mercy and find grace to help us in our time of need" (Hebrews 4:15, 16, *NIV*).

UNDERSTANDING WHAT YOU READ

In this section you should have discovered that there are certain clear indications that a person has been adopted into the family of God.

1. God gives the believer an _____ of the inheritance he is to receive.

2. Because we are sons, we have every right to live _____.

3. Because we are sons, we may have an _____ with the Father whenever we need to approach Him.

4. Christ takes our imperfect _____ and perfects them.

Answers, page 181.

We have talked mainly about the privileges and blessings of sonship, but there is a price to pay. If we are sons and therefore members of the family, we must live by the standards set for the family. There cannot be an inconsistency that allows one member of the family to enjoy privileges and rights that are denied other members. The standards for the family of God are the commands of God.

John wrote, "Everyone who believes that Jesus is the Christ is born of God, and everyone who loves the father loves his child as well. This is how we know that we love the children of God: by loving God and carrying out his commands. This is love for God: to obey his commands. And his commands are not burdensome" (1 John 5:1-3, *NIV*). By living in harmony with His will, we perform our responsibility as sons.

FOR FURTHER STUDY

Evans, William. *The Great Doctrines of the Bible.* Chicago: Moody, 1949.

SELF-CHECK TEST

After you have read Chapter 8 and looked up the verses in the Bible, you should take this brief self-check test. Answer the questions without referring back to the text.

True or False

Indicate whether each statement is True or False by witting "T" or "F" in the blank to the left.

_____ 1. The Apostle Paul was the only New Testament writer to develop the doctrine of adoption.

_____ 2. In Rome the adopted person gained only part of the rights of a full son.

_____ 3. Pharaoh's daughter kept Moses from infancy.

_____ 4. Believers are presently sons of God.

_____ 5. All believers enjoy all their privileges in Christ.

_____ 6. In this world we are not recognized as sons of God, but someday we shall throw off this disguise.

_____ 7. Jesus is described as being "the image of the invisible God."

_____ 8. God's love has no limits.

_____ 9. We should lose heart when we are disciplined.

_____ 10. There is no consistent standard for members of the family of God.

When you have marked the answers for these ten questions, look up the answers in the back of the book. If you got at least eight answers right, you may proceed to Chapter 9. If you had three or more wrong answers, you should read this lesson again, retake the test, and then go ahead to Chapter 9.

9

MEDIATION: A CHANGE OF ACCESS

C hrist's work for the believer did not end at Calvary or at conversion. The writer of Hebrews said, "He is able to save completely those who come to God through him, because he always lives to intercede for them" (7:25, *NIV*). This is a picture of Christ continuing His work. He did not cease to intervene for men when He passed into the heavens; He still pleads their case. His function as a high priest was not stopped at Calvary; He still fills that important role. Men who could not otherwise reach God have access to Him through Christ. Barclay termed this thought "the vision of a Christ who loved us from the first of time and who will love us to the

last, and whose continued love is our eternal hope of
soteria [salvation]."

Christ, Our High Priest

Looking again to the Book of Hebrews we read, "For
we do not have a high priest who is unable to sympathize
with our weaknesses, but we have one who has been
tempted in every way, just as we are—yet was without
sin. Let us then approach the throne of grace with confidence, so that we may receive mercy and find grace to
help us in our time of need" (Hebrews 4:15, 16, *NIV*).

Christ, our high priest, understands us and sympa-
thizes with us. He knows the weakness of the flesh
and deals tenderly with us.

Take the case of the woman caught in the act of
adultery (John 8). It is dawn in Jerusalem. Jesus is seated in the Temple court teaching the people. He is
rudely interrupted by teachers of the Law and the
Pharisees. They bring this woman in and make her
stand before the group as they tell Jesus that she was
caught in the act of adultery.

"Moses," they say, "commanded us to stone such
women. Now what do you say?" (v. 5, *NIV*). Their
question is designed to trap Him. But He wisely calls
upon anyone among the accusers who is without sin
to cast the first stone at her.

At that challenge they begin to walk away one at a
time until only Jesus is left with the woman. Then He
says to her, "Where are [your accusers]? Has no one
condemned you?" (v. 10, *NIV*).

She replies, "No one, Sir." (v. 11, *NIV*). Jesus assures
her that He does not condemn her. He tells her to go
and leave her life of sin.

As our high priest, Jesus is just as compassionate when we look to Him today. He is eager to help us and to strengthen us and to send us forth in the right direction.

Jesus has been tried in the same way we are tried; therefore, He can identify with us (Hebrews 4:15). He experienced all the physical problems that we know. He got hungry and tired. He also knew what it was like to have no place to lay His head (Luke 9:58). When we bring our needs to Him, He knows what our prayer is all about. He responds as One who has walked where we have walked.

Christ also knew mental anguish. The weight of the sins of the world rolled in on His shoulders, and He was described as "exceedingly sorrowful, even unto death" (Matthew 26:37). We have never felt such deep depression.

In Nazareth He was astonished at the unbelief of the people (Mark 6:1-6). His ministry was hindered because of their attitude. We have never been disappointed more in someone than was He.

Judas was trusted and befriended by the Lord. He was selected to take care of the treasury, as well as being numbered with the disciples. Although honored by the Lord in this way, he betrayed Christ. When we feel that we do not have a friend in the world, let us remember how Jesus was treated by this friend. He understands our feelings.

After Jesus had healed ten lepers, only one returned to thank Him (Luke 17:11-19). Imagine how He must have felt! When we are treated with ingratitude, He can identify with us.

To go a step further, Jesus also experienced spiritual distress. How else can His cry be explained: "My God, my God, why hast thou forsaken me?" (Matthew 27:46). Who can imagine the depths from which that cry came? How can we question our Christian experience and think that Christ does not understand? He knows exactly how we feel, and He is ready to help us make it through that trial.

We have every reason to rejoice because of our High Priest. Without Him our faltering steps would lead us to despair. But because of His grace, we can follow a steady course and come out victorious. He is our great hope and sustainer.

UNDERSTANDING WHAT YOU READ

In this section you should have discovered how completely Christ qualified for the role of high priest. As our intercessor He identifies with us.

1. Jesus told the woman caught in the act of adultery to _____ her life of sin.

2. We have never felt such deep _____ as did Jesus when the weight of the sin of the world rolled in on His shoulders.

3. Who can imagine the _____ out of which came the cry, "My God, my God, why hast thou forsaken me?"

Answers, page 182.

Christ, Our Intercessor

Has Christ ever prayed for us personally? We may say, "Not that I know of." Then maybe our case is like that of Simon Peter.

Peter, it seems, always spoke first, no matter what the subject was. When Jesus asked the disciples, "Who do you say 1 am?" it was Peter who answered. He said, "You are the Christ, the Son of the living God" (Matthew 16:15,16, *NIV*). When Jesus began to explain to His disciples that He must go to Jerusalem and suffer and die, it was Simon Peter who objected loudest (Matthew 16:21-23). He even took Jesus aside and rebuked Him for talking like that. He insisted that such a thing could never happen to the Lord. Then, when the end was nearing, it was Simon Peter who declared, "Lord, I am ready to go with you to prison and to death" (see Luke 22:31-34, *NIV*). In that setting Jesus revealed to Peter just how precarious his position was. It seems that Satan had been trying to bargain for Peter's soul. He wanted to take him and sift him as wheat. It seems Peter's disposition was such that Satan could have done just that with him. "But," said Jesus, "I have prayed for you, Simon, that your faith may not fail."

Let us take a close look at this picture. Satan was trying to destroy Simon Peter, but Peter was unaware of what Satan was doing. Jesus was aware of Satan's intentions; and He prayed for Simon Peter, although Peter did not know that Jesus was praying for him. Yet, it was that prayer that kept Peter's faith from failing.

How many times do we suppose that scene has been repeated for believers in every age? Satan sought to destroy them, but Jesus prayed for them; and they were delivered, although they were unaware of what was happening.

How many times has that scene been played out in

our life? We don't know. Nobody does. But I dare say it has happened in the life of every believer. When we look back on our life and remember some of the things that have happened, we know that we came through those moments only because the Lord was praying for us.

It is two o'clock in the morning. The lady is awakened from her sleep. She is troubled in her spirit. A feeling that her former pastor and his family are facing danger weighs heavily upon her. She kneels beside her bed and prays—for two hours. Then a calm assurance comes that everything is going to be all right. She is able to sleep again.

Now, it is ten o'clock that morning. The pastor's 16-year-old son calls and gets permission to drive the family car downtown. Within 30 minutes the phone rings again. This time it is the youngest daughter. The son has wrecked the car. No one was seriously hurt and the damages were minimal. Was the lady's prayer a factor?

No doubt her prayer was divinely prompted and perfected by the Lord Himself. In His intercessory role, Jesus took her petition to the Father . The result was that she had inner peace and harm was kept from the pastor's family.

Ours is an age of uncertainty. News reports leave a negative cast in our mind. Problems seem unsolvable. The best minds sometimes make the poorest judgment. From a natural standpoint there is not much to be hopeful about, but what a different perspective we have as believers! No matter how dark the scene is around us, we know that there is One who is praying for us. And with His help we can cope with every circumstance of life.

UNDERSTANDING WHAT YOU READ

In this section you should have discovered that the Lord is praying for you. No doubt, He has prayed for you when you were not aware of His prayer.

1. Satan wanted to _____ Simon Peter.
2. Jesus was aware of Satan's _____ , and prayed for Peter.
3. Looking back over our life, we know that we came through some things only because _____ was praying for us.
4. With Jesus' help we can _____ with every _____ of life.

Answers, page 182.

Christ, Our Advocate

Stephen was mightily used of God (Acts 6:5-8:2). Through him God performed great wonders and miracles among the people. Because of the Spirit-inspired wisdom by which he spoke, his opponents could not stand up to him. But some of them accused him of speaking words of blasphemy against Moses and against God. So they seized Stephen and brought him before the Sanhedrin Court. Stephen's enemies brought false witnesses who supported their charges. Even under attack Stephen's face shone like the face of an angel.

Stephen reflected the history of God's prophets and the ill treatment they had sometimes received at the hands of those who called themselves the people of God. When the members of the Sanhedrin heard what Stephen had to say, they were furious and gnashed their teeth at him. They covered their ears and yelled at the top of their voices; they took him and began to stone him. In the midst of this confusing scene on earth, there appeared to

Stephen a calm and reassuring scene in heaven. The curtains of heaven, as it were, were drawn back, and Stephen saw the glory of God and Jesus standing at the right hand of God. No wonder Stephen could pray the prayer that Jesus prayed on the Cross, "Lord, do not hold this sin against them" (*cf.* Luke 23:34).

Was Jesus watching over Stephen at this difficult moment in his life? Not only was he watching over him, but the Lord who is usually pictured as sitting at the right hand of God stood up in honor of His courageous servant. Jesus must have stood with outstretched arms indicating to Stephen that if men rejected him on earth, he was welcome in heaven. Encouraged by what he saw, Stephen could take the pelting of the stones and simply fell asleep.

"But," you say, "Stephen was a martyr; he deserved the attention the Lord gave him. What about me? I've never done anything to merit that kind of watch care." The Bible teaches that even the smallest act performed for the glory of the Lord comes to His awareness. If we give a cup of cold water to a disciple of the Lord, Christ takes note of it.

Jesus said, "He who receives you receives me, and he who receives me receives the one who sent me. Anyone who receives a prophet because he is a prophet will receive a prophet's reward, and anyone who receives a righteous man because he is a righteous man will receive a righteous man's reward. And if anyone gives a cup of cold water to one of these little ones because he is my disciple, I tell you the truth, he will certainly not lose his reward" (Matthew 10:40-42, *NIV*).

A certain local church needed to raise money to pay

some bills so the members started a candy project. They were both making and selling candy. One of the members was present for every work session. Other members who could be there, whose work load was about the same as the faithful member, never came. After several nights, this member began to complain about those who were not helping. The pastor reassured her. He told her that she had not made or sold one piece of candy (if she had done it with the right attitude) that had escaped the notice of the Lord. In His infinite goodness, God would reward her for all she had done. And He would do so just because He is who He is.

Every believer can be sure that anything he does with the right motive will be rewarded of the Lord. We do not do it for the reward; nevertheless, God still gives. The eye of the Lord is always on His people (Psalm 33:18); nothing we do ever escapes His attention.

UNDERSTANDING WHAT YOU READ

In this section you should have discovered that Jesus cares about you and that His watchful eye is upon you.

1. Jesus _____ over Stephen at the most difficult moment in his life.
2. The smallest _____ performed for the _____ of the Lord comes within the range of Jesus' awareness.
3. Anything the believer does with the right _____ will be rewarded of the Lord.

Answers, page 182.

Christ Keeps Us in His Power

In the Old Testament, there is a story about three Jews. Shadrach, Meshach, and Abednego were appointed to administrative posts in Babylon. Because they were committed to God, they refused to obey a decree from the king that all under his rule bow and worship an image of gold he had erected. The penalty for refusal was to be thrown into a blazing furnace. The king was furious when he learned of their defiance. When the three were brought before the king and threatened, they responded, "O Nebuchadnezzar, we do not need to defend ourselves before you in this matter. If we are thrown into the blazing furnace, the God we serve is able to save us from it, and he will rescue us from your hand, O king. But even if he does not, we want you to know, O king, that we will not serve your gods or worship the image of gold you have set up" (Daniel 3:16-18, NIV).

Nebuchadnezzar was so enraged by what he heard that he ordered the furnace heated seven times hotter than usual. He then commanded that the three Jews be bound and cast into the furnace, clothes and all. The furnace was so hot that the flames killed the men who threw them in. To the king's astonishment, when he looked into the furnace he saw four men walking around in the fire, unbound and unharmed. And the fourth man looked to him like "a son of the gods" (v. 25, NIV). So, the king freed the men from the furnace and decreed that anyone who spoke out against the God of Shadrach, Meshach, and Abednego would be "cut into pieces and their houses be turned into piles of rubble, for no other god can save in this way" (v. 29, NIV).

Even in Daniel's day, men who trusted in God knew

of His keeping power. The Apostle Paul learned this lesson well also. He wrote to Timothy, "I know whom I have believed, and am convinced that he is able to guard what I have entrusted to him for that day" (2 Timothy 1:12, *NIV*).

That trust in God was still intact when Paul came to the end of his journey. He wrote, "The time has come for my departure. I have fought the good fight, I have finished the race, I have kept the faith. Now there is in store for me the crown of righteousness, which the Lord, the righteous Judge, will award to me on that day—and not only to me, but also to all who have longed for his appearing" (2 Timothy 4:6-8, *NIV*).

Dr. Clarence Edward Macartney was one of the great ministers of the twentieth century. When he was near the end of his life, a visitor came to Dr. Macartney's home. The minister asked his guest to read from the Book of Job. He then called members of the family around and led in prayer as the home was filled with the music of the Psalter. Knowing that death drew near, he planned his funeral service to be a simple testimony of praise to Jesus Christ and His triumphant grace. He chose the hymns "Rock of Ages," "The Twenty-third Psalm," and "Amazing Grace" as a witness to his faith. His last message to his friends was, "Tell them my anchor still holds." He knew the keeping power of God.

Every believer can have the same hope these saints had. God not only saves us from our sins, but He keeps us by His power. He has a vested interest in us. It cost His Son His life that we might be saved. Is it not reasonable to expect that He will keep us?

"He that spared not his own Son, but delivered him up for us all, how shall he not with him also freely give us all things?" (Romans 8:32).

He is "able to keep you from falling, and to present you faultless before the presence of his glory with exceeding joy" (Jude 24).

UNDERSTANDING WHAT YOU READ

In this section you should have discovered that Jesus not only saves, but keeps us by His power.

1. Even in Daniel's day men who trusted in God knew of His _____ power.
2. Paul's _____ in God was still intact when he came to the end of his journey.
3. Is it not reasonable to expect that God will _____ us since He has done so much to redeem us?

Answers, page 182.

We have an Intercessor who is pleading our case at the right hand of the Father. His work there is a continuation of the results begun at Calvary. What blessed security we have in Him!

FOR FURTHER STUDY

Morris, Leon. *The Lord From Heaven*. Grove, IL: InterVarsity, 1974.

SELF-CHECK TEST

After you have read Chapter 9 and looked up the verses in the Bible, you should take this brief self-check test. Answer the questions without referring back to the text.

Explain how the following verses or questions apply to your life.

1. Hebrews 4:15,16 _____

_____

2. What do you have in common with Simon Peter's experience? _____

_____

3. What do you have in common with Stephen's experience? _____

_____

4. Matthew 10:40-42 _____

_____

5. What do you have in common with the three Hebrew children in Daniel's story? _____

_____

6. Hebrews 7:25 _____

_____

When you have marked your answers, go on to Chapter 10.

10

LIFESTYLE: A CHANGE OF CHARACTER

As believers our sins have been forgiven and we have been adopted into the family of God. Our citizenship is in heaven, and our lifestyle on earth should reflect this new status. From the beginning of our Christian journey, we should be determined to develop the characteristics of a believer and to "grow in grace, and in the knowledge of our Lord and Saviour, Jesus Christ" (2 Peter 3:18).

To begin to grow now and to continue to make progress will enable us to avoid the disappointment experienced by the artist who failed to reach his potential. The artist, according to Donald Grey Barnhouse, visited a museum where one of his masterpieces was on exhibition and saw one of his early paintings. He turned away from the comparison with sadness. A friend told him he should be pleased because of the progress he had made. The artist smiled sadly and replied that he was grieved because he had realized so little of the promise he had shown in his youth.

We have the challenge to show by our life a portrait of Jesus Christ to a world that so sorely needs a sight of Him. The life that will point men to Christ shows the fruit of the Spirit: "love, joy, peace, long-suffering, gentleness, goodness, faith, meekness, temperance: against such there is no law" (Galatians 5:22, 23). These fruit may be divided into three categories: fruit that reflects our personal feelings—love, joy, and peace; fruit that affects our relationship with others—long-suffering, gentleness, and goodness; fruit that makes known our attitude toward God—faith, meekness, and temperance.

Fruit That Reflects Our Personal Feelings

The centerpiece of the Christian life is love. The example for and source of that love is God. He is love (1 John 4:16), and therefore love is the greatest characteristic the believer can possess. Love is the cement that binds everything together in perfect harmony. Paul wrote, "Therefore, as God's chosen people, holy and dearly loved, clothe yourselves with compassion, kindness, humility, gentleness and patience. Bear with each other and forgive whatever grievances you may have against one another. Forgive as the Lord forgave you. And over all these virtues put on love, which binds them all together in perfect unity" (Colossians 3:12-14, *NIV*).

In *The Miracle of the Holy Spirit*, Charles L. Allen wrote,

"Once I was preaching in a revival in a small rural church. In one of the morning services, I invited people to give their own testimony, to tell what the Lord had done in their own lives. I shall never forget one man in particular. He had spent his life working a small farm. He was not educated in a formal way, but he gave one of the best descriptions of Christian love I have ever heard.

"He stood and said, 'When I was a little boy I loved my mother. As I grew older I felt I would never love anybody else but my mother. As a young man I met a girl and I came to love her and I married her. I then loved my mother and my wife but I knew I would never love anyone else. Then a baby boy was born into our home. As I held him in my arms, I knew that I loved him, too. We never had any other children and those were the only three people I loved. Then during a service here in this church, the Lord Jesus Christ came into my heart. When I came to know Jesus as my Savior, I loved Him. Then a strange thing happened. Loving my mother and my wife and my son did not cause me to love anybody else. But when I loved Jesus, then I loved everybody!'"

The distinguishing attitude of the believer is joy. Paul said, "Rejoice in the Lord always. I will say it again: Rejoice!" (Philippians 4:4, *NIV*). That is a large command. Did Paul mean that there is to be an underlying joy in all of our life? Was he implying that the glow on our face may be a witness for Christ? In all circumstances of life it is possible to have the strength of joy. When outsiders see our inner joy amid outward turmoil, they will be attracted to the Christ who makes that possible. In Him there is so much to rejoice about.

Do you remember the joy you experienced when you first believed? I was 12 years old when I came to Christ. The next day I felt like a little boy wearing a white suit. I was so excited about what God had done for me that I stood up in class at public school and testified about accepting Christ into my life. My zeal may have exceeded my wisdom, but there was no question about my joy. Maybe your experience was similar. Do you still have that joy? Has your joy in Christ grown through the years?

Joy is present at every turn of the Christian life. It is found in fulfilling the ministry the Lord has given to us, in fellowship with other believers, and in bringing someone to a saving knowledge of Christ. So strong is this joy that it undergirds the believer in times of sorrow or difficulty. What a way to witness for Christ!

Every relationship of the Christian life should be affected by inner peace. The forces we face every day in our world promote turmoil and confusion. At home, on the job, in school, at church . . . all our circumstances can bring frustration. But life should not and does not have to be lived that way. There is a peace based on the righteousness of Christ that enables us to build harmonious relationships in every aspect of life. Jesus has made that peace available to every believer, and by allowing Him to manifest His peace in our lives, we become effective witnesses for Him.

When Jesus spoke to His disciples about His departure, He told them, "Peace I leave with you; my peace I give you. I do not give to you as the world gives. Do not let your hearts be troubled and do not be afraid" (John 14:27, *NIV*). That same peace is still available to every believer.

Paul gave instructions in the fourth chapter of Philippians that, if followed, will result in peace. He spoke of living with joy, showing gentleness, knowing the Lord is near, overcoming anxiety, and praying about everything. He said if we live this way, "the peace of God, which transcends all understanding, will guard your hearts and minds in Christ Jesus" (Philippians 4:7, *NIV*).

UNDERSTANDING WHAT YOU READ

In this section you should have discovered the importance of love, joy, and peace in the life of a believer. These characteristics make life worth living.

1. Love is the cement that _____ everything together in perfect harmony.

2. When outsiders see our inner _____ amid outward _____ , they will be attracted to Christ.

3. Bringing someone to a _____ knowledge of Christ produces joy.

4. The peace of Christ is still available to every _____.

Answers, page 182.

Fruit That Affects Our Relationship With Others

Long-suffering is an important virtue that deserves to be cultivated. Barclay says that long-suffering "expresses the attitude to people which never loses patience with them, however unreasonable they may be, and which never loses hope for them, however unlovely and unteachable they may be. It expresses the attitude to events which never admits defeat, and which never loses its hope and its faith, however dark the situation may be, and however incomprehensible events may be, and however sore the chastening of God may be."

Long-suffering is a godlike characteristic. Every sinner knows that he deserves to be punished for his sin. Only because God is "not willing that any should perish, but that all should come to repentance" (2 Peter 3:9) do we know the joy of salvation. If God was short-tempered, we would all be lost! Because of His long-suffering, we all have hope.

This godlike trait is valuable in our dealings with other people. A person who has no patience with others will not have many friends and will see his influence evaporate. In *A Balanced Church*, Dr. Charles W. Conn wrote, "Sometimes we may have a tendency to 'write off' offensive persons, but when we do we go contrary to the example of Christ (Luke 14:9), Moses (Exodus 32:32), and Paul (Galatians 4:19, 20), who said: 'We then that are strong ought to bear the infirmities of the weak, and not to please ourselves' (Romans 15:1). We are to restore, not destroy, those who are weaker Christians than ourselves (Galatians 6:1)."

Another grace of character that every believer should manifest is gentleness. Elsewhere in the Scripture the word is translated *kindness*. It is that attitude that leads the Christian to treat others in the way in which God has treated him.

Will Rogers is credited with having said, "I never met a man I didn't like." I don't know what kind of people Rogers met, but I suspect that he met men of all dispositions and personalities. Some of them would have turned most people off, but not Will Rogers. His attitude says a lot about the man.

In *Memoirs of Childhood and Youth*, Albert Schweitzer wrote, "All ordinary violence produces its own limitations, for it calls forth an answering violence which sooner or later becomes its equal or superior. But kindness works simply and perseveringly; it produces no strained relations which prejudice its working, strained relations which already exist it relaxes. Mistrust and misunderstanding it puts to flight, and it strengthens itself by calling forth answering kindness. Hence it is furthest reaching and most effective of all forces."

It seems such a simple thing to be kind. A poor person needs a helping hand. How easy it is to give a little time and effort! And what a difference it may make in that life! An older person is lonely and in need. The smallest gesture will bring cheer and will give that person pleasant thoughts to share with his friends. A little child has stubbed a toe, or hurt a finger, or been bruised in some way. A kiss and a hug will chase away the pain and give the child happiness and joy.

Goodness is also a fruit of the Spirit. The least that can be said of someone is that he or she is a good person. I am not sure that we value this virtue in people. Our measurement of others too often is personality or achievement—shallow things compared to character. We sometimes lose sight of their insensitivity to others, their arrogance, their selfishness. On the other hand, the person who is low-key, not flashy, but good at heart we take for granted. This is unfortunate. Sometimes the accomplishments of that quieter person far outlast those of the more popular.

The lovely child Nell is one of Dickens' most beautiful characters. From infancy she was the victim of misfortune. Faithful to her aged grandparent who was a gambler by nature, Little Nell wandered to and fro over

England. She was often homeless and cold and came in
contact with coarse and rude men—gypsies, gamblers,
bargemen, furnacemen, and showmen. Yet, wherever
she went, she displayed a sweetness that awakened
kindness in others. Her attitude spoke to that better
angel that sleeps in every human heart. "When I die,"
was her request, "put near me some thing that has loved
the light, and had the sky above it always."

Everyone who read *The Old Curiosity Shop* must feel
the gentle warmness of this noble child, Little Nell.
And who would say that this lovely person lived in
vain? Or that her life of goodness was not profitable to
others? Who, indeed, can measure the reach and
impact of a good and godly life?

UNDERSTANDING WHAT YOU READ

In this section you should have discovered that long-suffering, gentleness, and goodness are essential to good relationships with other people.

1. Long-suffering never loses _____ with or
_____ for people.
2. We are to _____ , not destroy, those who are weaker
Christians than ourselves.
3. Kindness puts _____ and _____ to flight.
4. The least that can be said of someone is that he or she is
a _____ person.

Answers, page 182.

Fruit That Makes Known Our Attitude Toward God

*One fruit of the Spirit that shows a right attitude toward
God and man is faithfulness.* Although the Authorized
Version translates this word *faith*, most translators

agree that *faithfulness* is a better translation. "It describes," according to Barclay, "the man on whose faithful service we may rely, on whose loyalty we may depend, whose word we can unreservedly accept. It describes the man in whom there is the unswerving and inflexible fidelity of Jesus Christ, and the utter dependability of God."

Abraham was an Old Testament example of faithfulness. When God told him to leave his home country and go to a land that he would later receive as an inheritance, he faithfully obeyed. Abraham did not know where his journey would take him, but he knew that God would not fail him. He was content to be a stranger in a foreign land and to live in tents; such was his faithfulness to the Lord. He believed there was a city with foundations, whose architect and builder was God. Later, when Lot found himself in trouble in Sodom, it was the faithfulness of Abraham that God honored when he spared Lot as the city was destroyed.

The ultimate example of faithfulness and loyalty is Jesus Christ. He is referred to in the Book of Revelation as the faithful witness, the faithful and true (1:5; 19:11). He is also the merciful and faithful high priest (Hebrews 2:17). A single glimpse of Gethsemane will convince any objective mind of the faithfulness of Christ to God. Although He expressed the hope of a way whereby redemption could be secured, His prayer was, "Not my will, but thine, be done" (Luke 22:42).

Another attitude produced by the Spirit is meekness. Meekness may be defined as an accurate assessment of oneself. It avoids both the extreme of thinking we are more important or more capable than we really are and the extreme of thinking we have less ability and less worth than we actually have. It is the blessed experience of reaching a happy medium and applying that principle to every aspect of life.

Meekness is a characteristic that every leader should possess. It would give him the courage to act boldly and humility to wait upon God for guidance.

Meekness is a characteristic that every husband and wife should exercise. Then, there would be words of kindness and comfort in the home and not words of anger and disappointment. Then, the tone of the voice would be soft, gentle and low, not sharp and high-pitched.

Meekness is a characteristic every employer and employee should have. If so, there would be greater harmony and a unified effort to achieve common goals. How much could be accomplished in any place of employment if problems between management and labor were avoided and everybody made an effort to produce the best possible product?

Is there any characteristic that would do more for the good of man than meekness? It is a quality without which a man can never reach the heights God intended him to scale. It is one of the great essentials of life. It makes a man a king among men.

Also, temperance is a fruit of the Spirit that deals with attitude. In its scriptural use *temperance* means "self-control." It is that trait that comes to a man when Christ is in his heart, that characteristic that enables him to live and to walk in the world, and yet to keep his garments unspotted (James 1:27).

Solomon made two important statements about self-control: "Better a patient man than a warrior, a man who controls his temper than one who takes a city" (Proverbs 16:32, *NIV*). "Like a city whose walls are broken down is a man who lacks self-control" (Proverbs 25:28, *NIV*).

Self-control gives purpose and definition to life. It indicates that a person knows where he is headed. His intentions are well-defined in his own mind; thus, in an intelligent manner he can pursue his goals. Life is most effective when it is lived in an orderly fashion. When the Holy Spirit is the dominant force in our life, order becomes natural. He, the Spirit, is the essence of order and self-control.

UNDERSTANDING WHAT YOU READ

In this section you should have discovered the meaning of faithfulness, meekness, and temperance. These traits are important in our attitude toward God and man.

1. Jesus Christ is the ultimate example of _____ and _____ .

2. Meekness is the blessed experience of reaching a happy _____ in life.

3. Meekness makes a man a _____ among men.

4. In its scriptural use temperance means " _____ ."

5. Self-control gives _____ and _____ to life.

Answers, page 182.

Bearing the fruit of the Spirit is essential to a Christlike character. Living the Christ-life enables us to win the confidence of others and thus be effective disciples.

FOR FURTHER STUDY

Allen, Charles A. *The Miracle of the Holy Spirit.* Old Tappan, NJ: Revell, 1974.

Barclay, William. *Flesh and Spirit.* Grand Rapids, MI: Baker, 1976.

Conn, Charles W. *A Balanced Church.* Cleveland, TN: Pathway, 1975.

Sanderson, John W. *The Fruit of the Spirit.* Grand Rapids, MI: Zondervan, 1976.

SELF-CHECK TEST

After you have read Chapter 10 and looked up the verses in the Bible, you should take this brief self-check test. Answer the questions without referring back to the text.

True or False

Indicate whether each statement is True or False by writing "T" or "F" in the blank to the left.

_____ 1. The life that manifests the fruit of the Spirit points men to Christ.

_____ 2. The centerpiece of the Christian life is love.

_____ 3. It is not possible to have the strength of joy in all the circumstances of life.

_____ 4.Life does not and should not have to be
lived in frustration.

_____ 5. Long-suffering is short-tempered.

_____ 6. We are to restore, not destroy, those who are
weaker Christians than ourselves.

_____ 7. The least that can be said of a person is that
he or she is a good person.

_____ 8. Abraham was a poor Old Testament example of faithfulness.

_____ 9. Meekness may be defined as an accurate assessment of oneself.

_____10. The Holy Spirit is the essence of order and
self-control.

*When you have marked the answers to these ten ques-
tions, look up the answers in the back of the book. If you got
at least eight answers right, you may proceed to Chapter 11.
If you had three or more wrong answers, you should read
this lesson again, retake the test, and then go ahead to
Chapter 11.*

11

DISCIPLESHIP: A CHANGE OF MASTERS

A *disciple* is "a pupil or follower who helps to spread his master's teachings." The original or secular word carries with it the idea of apprenticeship, similar to an apprentice in a trade like carpentry. Jesus said in Luke 6:40, "A student [disciple] is not above his teacher, but everyone who is fully trained will be like his teacher" (*NIV*). When fully discipled, His followers were to be like Him, despite their different personalities.

The disciple in Christianity is a follower of Jesus Christ, desiring to learn His ways and apply them to his life. It has been said that the one common trait that each of Jesus' 12 disciples had was that they were teachable.

A disciple has to be open and have a desire to learn.

The Disciple and Prayer

In his book *How to Pray*, R. A. Torrey lists 11 reasons why it is important to pray. First, because there is a devil. Paul said, "Our struggle is not against flesh and blood, but against . . . the spiritual forces of evil in the heavenly realms. Therefore put on the full armor of God. . . . And pray in the Spirit on all occasions with all kinds of prayers and request" (Ephesians 6:12-18, *NIV*).

Next, prayer is God's appointed way for obtaining things. The reason we lack anything in our life and in our work is neglect of prayer. "You do not have, because you do not ask God. When you ask, you do not receive, because you ask with wrong motives" (James 4:2, 3, *NIV*).

Then, those men whom God set forth as an example of what He expects Christians to be—the apostles— regarded prayer as the most important aspect of their life. When the responsibilities of the early church grew and started crowding in upon the disciples, they called the multitude together and said that it was not right that they should leave the disciples of God to serve tables. So they appointed seven godly men to take care of those matters so that the apostles could give themselves "continually to prayer, and to the ministry of the word" (Acts 6:4).

Prayer played an important part in the earthly life of our Lord. Prayer took much of His time and strength. Thus, a man or woman who does not spend much time in prayer cannot properly be called a follower of Jesus Christ.

Praying is an important part of the present ministry of our risen Lord. Hebrews 7:25 says, "He is able to save . . . because he always lives to intercede for them" (NIV).

Also, as Hebrews 4:16 points out, prayer is the means that God has provided for our receiving mercy and obtaining the grace to help in the time of need.

And through prayer the disciple gains fullness of joy. "Ask and you will receive, and your joy will be complete" (John 16:24, NIV).

Prayer is the means for our obtaining freedom from anxiety and worry. Paul said, "Do not be anxious about anything, but in everything, by prayer and petition, with thanksgiving, present your requests to God. And the peace of God, which transcends all understanding, will guard your hearts and your minds in Christ Jesus" (Philippians 4:6, 7, NIV).

Through prayer we obtain the Holy Spirit. "If you then, though you are evil, know how to give good gifts to your children, how much more will your Father in heaven give the Holy Spirit to those who ask him!" (Luke 11:13, NIV).

Through prayer we overcome the temptations of this life, so that the day of Christ's return does not come upon us suddenly as a snare. (See Luke 21:34-36.)

Finally, prayer is important because of what it accomplishes. Much has been said about this already, but much needs to be added.

Prayer promotes spiritual growth as almost nothing else, indeed as nothing else but Bible study; and true Bible study and true prayer go hand in hand. It is through prayer that sin is brought to light, even the most hidden sin. The psalmist said, "Search me, O God, and know my heart: try me, and know my thoughts: And see if there be any wicked way in me" (Psalm 139:23, 24). When God shoots the penetrating rays of His light into the innermost recesses of the heart, sins never suspected are brought into view. In answer to prayer, God washes away evil and cleanses one's sins. In answer to prayer, eyes are opened to view wondrous truths out of God's Word. In answer to prayer, wisdom is obtained to know God's way and the strength to walk in it. As a disciple meets God in prayer and gazes into His face, he is changed into His image from glory to glory (2 Corinthians 3:18). Each day of true prayer life finds the disciples more like Jesus.

And it is through prayer that power is brought into the life of the disciple of Christ. Consider John Livingstone, who spent a night with others like him in prayer to God, and when he preached the next day in the Kirk of Shotts, 500 people were converted. If we want power for any work to which God calls us, be it preaching, teaching, personal work, or rearing children, we can get it by earnest prayer. Prayer and power are inseparable.

Prayer is used for the conversion of others. By prayer the bitterest enemies of the gospel have become its most valiant defenders; the greatest scoundrels have become the truest sons of God; and the vilest women have become the purest saints. It is the power of prayer to reach down where hope itself seems vain and lift men and women up into fellowship with and likeness to God.

A life of discipleship must have at its base a life of prayer. It is the foundation of Christian growth, the learning of God's will, and the attainment of a likeness to Christ.

UNDERSTANDING WHAT YOU READ

1. Prayer is important because there is a _____ against whom we battle.
2. Prayer is the means for our obtaining freedom from _____.
3. Prayer promotes spiritual growth as nothing else but _____.
4. Each day of true prayer life finds the disciples more like _____.

Answers, page 183.

The Disciple and the Word

It is through the Bible that God reveals Himself to mankind. In it are contained all the things that we need to know for faith and practice. It is God's final word to man about living in this world and knowing that we have eternal life.

To grow as disciples, it is important that we demonstrate faithfulness and a desire to learn and apply the Word of God. This may be done through hearing it preached and taught, reading it often, studying it, memorizing it, and meditating on the Scriptures.

James said that God "chose to give us birth through the word of truth, that we might be a kind of firstfruits of all he created" (James 1:18, *NIV*). It is through the Bible that the God of salvation is revealed to man. The New Birth comes through this Word of Truth. The

Bible clearly tells us that everything that has been written in it was "to teach us, so that through endurance and the encouragement of the Scriptures we might have hope" (Romans 15:4, *NIV*). And the biblical concept of hope has in it a sense of certainty, of knowing that we have eternal life with God.

To be a disciple is to lead a pure life; to lead a pure life is to be aware of sin. The only way that we can be aware of sin is to know the Word of God, which helps us to recognize sin in its many forms. The psalmist asked, "How can a young man keep his way pure?" And he answered, "By living according to your word. I seek you with all my heart; do not let me stray from your commands. I have hidden your word in my heart that I might not sin against you" (Psalm 119:9-11, *NIV*).

If the Christian disciple does not grow spiritually, he is stagnating and is not really a disciple. The Bible, however, enables us to grow spiritually. Our spiritual growth comes from taking in the Word of God as our spiritual food. The Bible guides and directs us through life. God has promised to lead, but to know what God has for us, we must be in the Word. "Trust in the Lord with all your heart and lean not on your own understanding; in all your ways acknowledge him, and he will make your paths straight" (Proverbs 3:5, 6, *NIV*).

Another reason the disciple should know the Word of God is to be an effective witness for Christ. No one can be an effective witness for the Savior unless he knows the Scripture; he has to have something to say to the unbelievers.

Ananias, speaking to Paul in Acts 22:14, 15, prophesied, "The God of our fathers has chosen you to know his will and to see the Righteous One and to hear words from his mouth. You will be his witness to all men of what you have seen and heard" (*NIV*).

So Paul wrote in 2 Corinthians 5:19, 20, that "God was reconciling the world to himself in Christ, not counting men's sins against them. And he has committed to us the message of reconciliation. We are therefore Christ's ambassadors, as though God were making his appeal through us. We implore you on Christ's behalf: Be reconciled to God" (*NIV*). God has given us the Bible that we might be effective witnesses for Him.

Finally, the Bible teaches us to live the life of a disciple of Christ. Paul said in 2 Timothy 3:16, 17, "All Scripture is God-breathed and is useful for teaching, rebuking, correcting and training in righteousness, so that the man of God may be thoroughly equipped for every good work" (*NIV*).

A disciple needs teaching. For Christian disciples teaching must come from the Word of God. Everything in the Christian life—our character, our words, our actions, our experience—is related to biblical teaching or doctrine. The Scripture is what we believe in and, it tells us what we are to do; it is the basis of our faith, its very foundation.

A disciple needs correction. A disciple needs the Scriptures to reveal how he has sinned and how he has missed the mark. The Bible serves as a mirror to show exactly what the disciple is like. The Bible not only tells us we have sinned, but also provides the corrective steps necessary for restoring fellowship with God and our fellow man. In other words, the Bible tells us how we can get back to where we ought to be in the life of discipleship.

A disciple also needs training in righteousness. The Bible tells us how to live a life pleasing to God, how to live harmoniously with our fellow man, and how to live in this world, which is under the domination of the evil one.

UNDERSTANDING WHAT YOU READ

1. Through the Bible God reveals Himself to _____.
2. To have a pure life one must be aware of _____.
3. The Bible _____ and _____ through life.
4. The Bible serves as a _____ to show exactly what the disciple is like.

Answers, page 183.

The Disciple and the Church

The church was all-important to Jesus. Paul emphasized this truth when he said that Christ loved His church "and gave himself up for her" (Ephesians 5:25, *NIV*). If Christ gave such a significant place to the church and repeatedly commissioned it to evangelize the world, it would benefit the disciple of Christ to seek daily a truer and deeper church sense.

A church is a fellowship with other Christian believers. A church makes one of its finest contributions to a Christian by providing a harmonious atmosphere in which to worship. A fellowship also causes mutual concern. It is part of the Christian nature to be concerned about others. When we are truly concerned, we share our time and energy with those who need us. Jesus said, "Inasmuch as ye have done it unto one of the least of these my brethren, ye have done it unto me" (Matthew 25:40). A fellowship cultivates love. A

Christian disciple is characterized by love. But love does not come easy to man; it must be cultivated. It grows as it is practiced in the fellowship of other Christians. A fellowship resolves differences. When changed men begin acting like their Heavenly Father, differences disappear. When individuals imitate Christ, the fellowship of the church, as well as the Christian disciple, moves in the direction God would have it to go.

A church magnifies worship. Worship is making a loving, obedient response to God's presence and recognizing His holiness and majesty. True worship takes place in an atmosphere conducive for approaching God with an earnest spirit. Proper surroundings, attitude, and actions are essential for effective worship experiences; and it is through the church that these conditions are to be met as it provides a place of worship for the disciple.

A church witnesses to the world. It is the duty of the Christian disciple to be a witness for Christ. Witnessing can come in many ways—personal witnessing, rearing one's children, always having a Christian smile—but one of the greatest witnesses is the church. Any work done for the church promotes the church as a witness for Christ and builds up the believer and makes him a better disciple.

A church educates. The work of the church does not end in introducing men to the Savior. That is like limiting the physician's role to delivering babies. A newborn Christian is a baby also, and the church is a home where he can grow up. To educate is to lead people to a knowledge and an acceptance of the

Christian faith and life, to train church members to perform the functions of a church, and to motivate them in Christian living and service.

Through a well-rounded church program, a disciple will find many services and activities that will help him learn and grow. And he will find a place where he can help others grow, producing more and more disciples.

UNDERSTANDING WHAT YOU READ

1. A Christian disciple is characterized by _____.

2. The church provides a place of _____ for the disciple.

3. It is the duty of the Christian disciple to be a _____ for Christ.

4. The church is a _____ where newborn Christians can grow up.

Answers, page 183.

The Disciple and Stewardship

A *steward* is "one called to exercise responsible care over possessions entrusted to him." A Christian disciple is to be a steward and is responsible for sharing his time, talent, and material possessions in the service of God and for the benefit of all mankind.

"Behold, the heaven and the heaven of heavens is the Lord's . . . the earth also, with all that therein is" (Deuteronomy 10:14). God owns our house, our car, our clothes, and even the air that we breathe. Everything that is belongs to God. And God has left us in charge of it all. We are God's stewards and are to exercise care over the possessions entrusted to us.

But we are not without guidelines to follow in this

stewardship. Tithing is the method that we use as a token of our recognition of God as the giver of all that we possess. "The tithe . . . is holy unto the Lord" (Leviticus 27:30) .

Withholding tithes and offering is robbing God (Malachi 3:8). But those who do tithe have God's blessing. "Bring ye all the tithes into the storehouse . . . and prove me now herewith, saith the Lord of hosts, if I will not open you the windows of heaven, and pour you out a blessing, that there shall not be room enough to receive it" (Malachi 3:10).

Tithing helps us to become glowing, growing Christians. Through tithing we learn that material values are secondary to spiritual values; we gain a broadening vision of the meaning of Christ's program in the world; and we increasingly become dedicated to that program. Christ's interests more and more become our own interests.

But our responsibility as stewards does not stop at tithing. All of our money is holy unto the Lord. Therefore we should take time and much thought before deciding how our money should be used. The way we earn our money, the way we spend our money, and the attitude we have concerning our money determines whether we are dishonoring Him who gives us the power to obtain wealth or whether we as faithful stewards are investing in the Lord's living causes and bearing fruitful testimony for Him.

Robert H. Hastings said, "One who is a good steward dollar-wise is more often than not a good steward of all 'the manifold grace of God' (1 Peter 4:10)."

UNDERSTANDING WHAT YOU READ

1. God owns _____.
2. Withholding tithes and offerings is _____ God.
3. Through tithing we learn that _____ values are secondary to _____ values.
4. All of our money is _____ unto the Lord.

Answers, page 183.

FOR FURTHER STUDY

Torrey, R. A. *How to Pray*. Chicago: Moody.

Sherrill, John. *My Friend, the Bible*. Lincoln, VA: Chosen, 1978.

Jefferson, C. E. *The Building of the Church*. Grand Rapids, MI: Baker, 1969.

Ely, Virginia. *Stewardship: Witnessing for Christ*. Westwood, NJ: Revell, 1962.

SELF-CHECK TEST

After you have read Chapter 11 and looked up the verses in the Bible, you should take this brief self-check test. Answer the questions without referring back to the text.

1. List four reasons why prayer is important to a disciple:

   _____

   _____

   _____

   _____

2. How does the Bible teach us to live the life of a disciple of Christ?

_____

_____

_____

3. Name three reasons why the church is important to the disciple:

_____

_____

_____

4. How is a disciple supposed to be a steward of his Master?

_____

_____

_____

When you have completed these nine possible answers, look up the correct responses in the back of the book. If you got at least seven answers right, you may proceed to Chapter 12. If you had three or more wrong answers, you should read this lesson again, retake the test, and then go ahead to Chapter 12.

12

GLORIFICATION: A CHANGE OF BODY

"For the Lord himself will come down from heaven . . . and the dead in Christ will rise first. After that, we who are still alive and are left will be caught up with them in the clouds to meet the Lord in the air.... and what we will be has not yet been made known. But we know that when he appears, we shall be like him" (1 Thessalonians 4:16, 17; 1 John 3:2, *NIV*).

What Men Will Become

Looking at a small acorn, who would ever see the mighty oak it might become? Who could dream of the power and majesty that acorn might see? Such a small and insignificant thing could surely have no value. But when the acorn is planted and subjected to death, it is given life: life more abundant. It reaches heights never before imagined. It becomes alive in a deeper, richer sense. The mighty oak looks nothing like an acorn, but that is what it once was. No one can see an oak tree by looking at an acorn, and no one can see what the believer is to become by looking at him now. Indeed, we cannot begin to fathom the fullness and completeness we shall know when we are transformed into the heavenly man.

Several important characteristics of the body we are to obtain are seen in Jesus' transfiguration (Matthew 17), His resurrected body (John 20; 21), and His appearance to John the Revelator (Revelation 1).

During His ministry Jesus once took Peter, James, and John upon a high mountain where He was transfigured before them. There these three disciples caught a glimpse of what the believer is to become. They saw the glory of Jesus. His face shone with light as bright as the sun, and His clothes became shining white beyond any white we know. Throughout the Bible, God is always spoken of in terms of light. It is truly the Son of God we see here, and we are to be like the Son of God. The purity of Jesus is shown in this scene. White symbolizes purity, and this is a whiter white than we can imagine. We are to be like the Son of God, and we are to be purer than even our greatest measure of purity. The spirituality of the body to come is also seen here. Our natural body is not well enough equipped to embody the Spirit of God as will be the new body we are to have. Our spiritual body will allow the light of God to shine forth from us.

After Jesus died, He was raised into the spiritual body. In the account of Jesus' life between His resurrection and ascension, three more characteristics of the spiritual body are shown. It is a powerful body, freed of limitations. This aspect was shown when Jesus came through a locked door to be with the disciples (John 20:19). The disciples were frightened at seeing Jesus, thinking Him to be a ghost. He took food and ate, proving that He was real. The body we are to inhabit will be a real body (Luke 24:39). Finally, we shall be recognized. Although the heavenly body will be different from the earthly body in many ways, we shall still be the same person. We shall be ourselves, and we shall be recognized as being ourselves. After His resurrection the disciples recognized Jesus (Luke 24:31). Jesus' body was powerful, real, and recognizable, and we shall be like Him.

In the first chapter of the Revelation, Jesus is seen in much the same way as He was seen at His transfiguration. Again, we see His glory and purity shown in terms of whiteness and light. There is, however, another aspect of our future body in this passage: "His head and hair were white like wool, as white as snow" (Revelation 1:14, *NIV*). This shows a picture of age. Jesus is immensely aged in the sense that He is eternal, and we shall be like Him.

Although some clues have been given through Jesus, we cannot begin to imagine all that God has in store for us in our spiritual bodies. Who would have ever thought there was an oak tree in that acorn?

UNDERSTANDING WHAT YOU READ

In this section you should have learned what men are to become.

1. On what three occasions did we see characteristics of a spiritual body?

   _____

   _____

   _____

2. God is seen throughout the Bible in terms of _____.
3. White symbolizes _____.

Answers, page 183.

Rewards

"No eye has seen, no ear has heard, no mind has conceived what God has prepared for those who love him" (1 Corinthians 2:9, *NIV*).

The idea of rewards is held throughout the Bible. In the story of Esther, Mordecai was rewarded for spoiling a plot to assassinate the king. He was given a kingly robe and was paraded through the city. He was also given a ring by the king, signifying authority.

Abraham was rewarded for his faith. God blessed his seed, choosing Abraham's descendants as His chosen people and bringing His Son into this world through Abraham's lineage. God blessed Job also. Job remained faithful to God through the most difficult of circumstances, and because of that God blessed him richly.

We, as believers, have been promised rewards. We have been promised a spiritual body that will shine forth as the sun and that will not be subject to death. We are to receive an eternal life of joy and gladness—

joy because we shall be complete. We shall experience the joy of fulfilling our destiny, the joy of seeing God and dwelling in His presence. We shall be called the children of God, heirs of God and joint heirs with Jesus. All things will be ours because we shall be heirs to the Owner of all things (Psalm 24:1).

We are sure of these rewards. God promised to give them to us. But there are even more rewards, more than we can imagine. Many rewards will be a direct result of our work here in this life. Jesus admonished us to lay up treasures in heaven. In several parables Jesus rewarded those who had been faithful, according to their works.

Our sins will be cast into the sea of forgetfulness, and all our works will be tested as by fire, destroying all unproductive work (1 Corinthians 3). For what is left, we shall be rewarded. It is frightening and awe-inspiring to consider that the only portions of our life to be remembered are those portions spent furthering the kingdom of God. It is comforting to know that all of our work for God will be rewarded beyond our wildest dreams.

UNDERSTANDING WHAT YOU READ

In this section you should have learned of the rewards God has in store for His children.

1. _____was rewarded for spoiling an assassination attempt.
2. Christians will enjoy _____ life.
3. Many rewards will be the direct result of our _____.

Answers, page 183.

Heaven

"I am going there to prepare a place for you" (John 14:2, *NIV*).

Jesus ascended into heaven to prepare a place for us in the presence of God. Heaven is a place. If it were not so, Jesus would have told us. Heaven is real.

In the Revelation John saw heaven as a tabernacle, as a city, and as a garden. As a tabernacle, heaven is the home of God. It is the most beautiful of cities. Indeed, no city can compare to it. It was also seen as a garden. This gives the idea of beauty, tranquility, and life.

Heaven is a holy place. (Read Revelation 21 and 22.) It is the home of God. Nothing will enter it that defiles in any way. It is a place of great beauty and great joy. There will be no tears, no sorrow, no death, no crying, and no pain. It is a place of holy delights and wonders. There is no night in heaven; yet, it has no need of a sun for the glory of God will light it.

The job of those who dwell in heaven is doing God's will. This activity includes many different things. We shall worship God and serve Him. Many saints will be given authority, as was shown in some of the parables Jesus told. (See Matthew 25:14-30.) There will be fellowship among the redeemed and fellowship with God. And finally, there will be rest, blessed rest from our labors.

Jesus went to prepare a wonderful place just for us. There is perfect security, no more fear. It is perfectly governed, for God is enthroned in heaven. The redeemed will have perfect knowledge and victory.

It is impossible to imagine the glories in store for

those who love the Lord. Heaven is the perfect place, where we shall know perfect joy and gladness. Heaven is the home of God, and we shall live in His presence.

UNDERSTANDING WHAT YOU READ

In this section you should have learned that heaven was prepared for us by Jesus.

1. John saw heaven in what three ways?

_____

_____

_____

2. Heaven is the home of _____.
3. The job of those who dwell in heaven is _____.

Answers, page 183.

Heaven on Earth

One of the most beautiful aspects of Christianity is that it is intended to improve the Christian and give him peace and happiness. We can enjoy heaven while we are yet on this earth.

God is omnipresent; thus, we can dwell in Him and He in us while we journey through life. Being in the presence of God is the greatest, most appealing characteristic of heaven. Anyone who has felt the presence of God in his life has tasted heaven. He wants a stronger taste and more of it. Evil men love darkness because their deeds are evil (John 3:19); but the righteous dwell in the light, for Jesus is the light of the world (John 8:12). Jesus is also the light of heaven (Revelation 21:23); thus, again we can experience heaven here on earth.

In heaven we are privileged to be able to see God. Those among us who are walking close to Him see Him in everything, for God is everywhere.

Jesus prayed to the Father, "Your will be done on earth as it is in heaven" (Matthew 6:10, *NIV*). Here we find the key to bringing heaven into our life. In heaven the will of God is done; when we do the will of God, we shall find ourselves in heaven. We shall be filled with love, and we shall know no fear, since there is no fear in love. We shall be at peace with God, with nature, with others, and even with ourselves. Our life will be filled with joy. There is the joy of knowing our destiny and working to fulfill it. There is the joy of doing the work of God. Surely, the greatest joy a Christian can ever feel, in heaven or on earth, is being the vessel God chooses to use to save another soul from eternal damnation.

Heaven will be ours for eternity, but it is also ours now. We are meant to live in the presence of God now and forever.

By obeying God and accepting Jesus we are transformed from a person of fears and limitations into a vessel of God's power. We are no longer a horror to God or to ourselves. We know only love for Him and His creation. We lose the selfish nature we were born with, and we do to others everything we would like them to do for us because we are so filled with the love of God. No longer must we be slaves to sin. We are allowed to go free from those ugly chains that held us for so long. We are given our freedom. Love is no longer missing in our life. We walk with God and He directs our paths.

With God in us we are made alive. Although we were doomed to death physically, morally, and spiritually, we are given life. We are no longer decaying morally; we are drawing closer to our Father spiritually, and we need not fear physical death anymore.

We choose between heaven and hell while we live here on earth. If we choose heaven now, we shall feel the presence of God for the rest of our life and for all eternity.

UNDERSTANDING WHAT YOU READ

In this section you should have learned that heaven is meant to be enjoyed while we are yet on this earth.

1._____ is the most appealing quality of heaven.

2. The key to bring heaven into our life is _____.

3. By obeying God we are no longer _____ to sin.

4. With God in us we are made _____.

Answers, page 183.

FOR FURTHER STUDY

Smith, Wilbur M. *The Biblical Doctrine of Heaven*. Chicago: Moody, 1969.

Summers, Ray. *The Life Beyond*. Nashville, TN: Broadman, 1959.

SELF-CHECK TEST

*After you have read Chapter 12 and looked up the verses
in the Bible, you should take this brief self-check test.
Answer the questions without referring back to the text.*

Multiple Choice

Circle the letter that indicates the answer that completes the following statements or record your
answers on another sheet of paper.

1. When Jesus appears . . .

    a. many will be killed.

    b. He will meet us on the ground.

    c. we shall be like Him.

    d. those living will go up to heaven first.

2. At the transfiguration of Jesus we see . . .

    a. His glory.

    b. His incorruptible purity.

    c. His spirituality.

    d. All of the above

3. After Jesus was raised from the dead, His body . . .

    a. was like that of a ghost.

    b. was real.

    c. was transparent.

    d. lacked the nail scars.

4. The picture of Jesus in the Revelation is . . .

    a. one of age.

    b. one of beauty.

    c. nothing like Jesus at His transfiguration.

    d. one of youth.

5. Abraham was rewarded for his . . .

    a. knowledge.

    b. sinlessness.

    c. good sense of humor.

    d. faith.

6. We have been promised a spiritual body . . .

    a. that is subject to death.

    b. that we shall not even recognize as being ourselves.

    c. that will shine forth as the sun.

    d. that has a good sense of humor.

7. Heaven will be illuminated by . . .

    a. fire.

    b. the glory of God.

    c. the sun.

    d. the moon.

8. Heaven is the perfect environment for . . .

    a. sinners.

    b. people with a good sense of humor.

    c. trees.

    d. believers.

When you have marked the answers to these eight questions, look up the answers in the back of the book. If you had three or more wrong answers, you should read this lesson again, and retake the test.

ANSWER KEYS

for

Understanding what you Read

and Self-Check Tests

ANSWER KEY
Understanding What You Read

CHAPTER ONE
Section 1, Page 15
1. rule
2. the Garden of Eden
3. woman
4. the tree of the knowledge of good and evil

Section 2, Page 19
1. serpent
2. they were naked
3. the serpent, woman, man
4. the fruit of the tree of life

Section 3, Page 23
1. animals
2. die
3. love

CHAPTER TWO
Section 1, Page 29
1. feeding pigs
2. hired servant
3. ran to meet him
4. alive

Section 2, Page 32
1. the house of Israel
2. his son
3. killed
4. religious leaders

Section 3, Page 35
1. rejected Him
2. business
3. Gentiles
4. happy

ANSWER KEY
Understanding What You Read

CHAPTER THREE
Section 1, Page 42
1. Isaac's sacrifice, the lifting up of the brazen serpent
2. prophets, angels
3. redemption

Section 2, Page 45
1. Sin
2. Calvary
3. love
4. means

Section 3, Page 47
1. takes, accord
2. infinite, finite
3. holiness
4. necessary

Section 4, Page 50
1. universal, limited
2. limited, accepted
3. child

CHAPTER FOUR
Section 1, Page 57
1. God
2. Pharisee, publican
3. lightly, breaks
4. Restitution

Section 2, Page 60
1. sorrow
2. sin
3. turning
4. Cross

Section 3, Page 63
1. rejoicing
2. forgiveness, pardon
3. broken heart

ANSWER KEY
Understanding What You Read

CHAPTER FIVE
Section 1, Page 70
1. first
2. right
3. lack
4. obtain

Section 2, Page 72
1. Word
2. Paul
3. knowledge
4. Christ

Section 3, Page 75
1. grace
2. author, perfecter
3. Word
4. Prayer

Section 4, Page 77
1. faith
2. development
3. watchful care

CHAPTER SIX
Section 1, Page 85
1. citizenship
2. Onesimus
3. sinned

Section 2, Page 89
1. aspect
2. justification
3. sin, mountain, sacrifice, heaven
4. for, by

Section 3, Page 91
1. favor
2. position
3. heir, joint heir

ANSWER KEY
Understanding What You Read

CHAPTER SEVEN
Section 1, Page 99
1. Christ
2. sinful, holiness
3. please, inherit
4. lost

Section 2, Page 103
1. new, divine
2. new nature
3. production
4. reformation, baptism

Section 3, Page 105
1. Believe
2. creative, reforming
3. death, resurrection
4. the Holy Spirit

Section 4, Page 107
1. children
2. sin, righteousness
3. flesh
4. attitude

CHAPTER EIGHT
Section 1, Page 112
1. position, advantages
2. son
3. Moses

Section 2, Page 115
1. long ago
2. moment
3. coming
4. lives

Section 3, Page 118
1. identify
2. nurture
3. family
4. console, discipline

Section 4, Page 120
1. earnest
2. confidently
3. audience
4. prayers

ANSWER KEY
Understanding What You Read

CHAPTER NINE
Section 1, Page 126
1. leave
2. depression
3. distress

Section 2, Page 129
1. destroy
2. intentions
3. Jesus
4. cope, circumstance

Section 3, Page 131
1. watched
2. act, glory
3. motive

Section 4, Page 134
1. keeping
2. trust
3. keep

CHAPTER TEN
Section 1, Page 141
1. binds
2. peace, turmoil
3. saving
4. believer

Section 2, Page 144
1. patience, hope
2. restore
3. mistrust, misunderstanding
4. good

Section 3, Page 147
1. faithfulness, loyalty
2. medium
3. king
4. self-control
5. purpose, definition

ANSWER KEY
Understanding What You Read

CHAPTER ELEVEN
Section 1, Page 155
1. devil
2. anxiety
3. Bible study
4. Jesus

Section 2, Page 158
1. mankind
2. sin
3. guides, directs
4. mirror

Section 3, Page 160
1. love
2. worship
3. witness
4. home

Section 4, Page 162
1. everything
2. robbing
3. material, spiritual
4. holy

CHAPTER TWELVE
Section 1, Page 168
1. (a) Jesus transfigured
   (b) Jesus risen
   (c) Jesus revealed to John
2. light
3. purity

Section 2, Page 169
1. Mordecai
2. eternal
3. works

Section 3, Page 171
1. (a) as a tabernacle
   (b) as a city
   (c) as a garden
2. God
3. doing God's will

Section 4, Page 173
1. Being in the presence of God
2. doing the will of God
3. slaves
4. alive

ANSWER KEY
Self-Check Tests

CHAPTER ONE
1. b   6. c
2. d   7. a
3. a   8. c
4. d   9. d
5. c   10. a

CHAPTER TWO
1. c   6. d
2. a   7. b
3. d   8. c
4. b   9. c
5. a   10. d

CHAPTER FOUR
1. Matthew 3:1,2; Matthew 4:17; Luke 24:45-47; 2 Peter 3:9
2. Psalm 51:1, 3, 4; Psalm 32:3-5
3. 2 Corinthians 7:9, 10; Isaiah 55:7; Proverbs 28:13
4. Acts 26:18; 1 Thessalonians 1:9; Isaiah 55:1-3
5. Luke 15:7, 10; Acts 2:38

CHAPTER FIVE
1. T   6. T
2. F   7. T
3. T   8. F
4. F   9. T
5. F   10. F

CHAPTER SIX
1. a. Forgiveness
   b. Restoration to favor with God
   c. Imputation of the righteousness of Christ
2. a. Keeping the Law
   b. Good deeds or conduct
3. a. The grace of God
   b. The blood of Christ
   c. Faith
4. a. The resurrection of Christ
   b. The gift of the Holy Spirit
5. a. Forgiveness
   b. Restoration to favor with God
   c. Imputation of the righteousness of Christ
   d. Sonship

ANSWER KEY
Self-Check Tests

CHAPTER SEVEN

1. F   6. F
2. T   7. T
3. T   8. T
4. F   9. F
5. F   10. F

CHAPTER EIGHT

1. T   6. T
2. F   7. T
3. F   8. T
4. T   9. F
5. F   10. F

CHAPTER TEN

1. T   6. T
2. T   7. T
3. F   8. F
4. T   9. T
5. F   10. T

CHAPTER ELEVEN

1. (a) There is a devil.
   (b) Through it we obtain fullness of joy.
   (c) Through it we obtain the Holy Spirit.
   (d) Because of what it accomplishes
2. By basing our life on prayer and the Word of God
3. (a) The church offers fellowship.
   (b) The church magnifies worship.
   (c) The church educates the believer.
4. A disciple is responsible for sharing his time, talent, and material possessions in the service of God and for the benefit of all mankind.

CHAPTER TWELVE

1. c   5. d
2. d   6. c
3. b   7. b
4. a   8. d